This book presents an abridged statement
of the author's trilogy:

The Foundations of Judaism: Method, Teleology, Doctrine.
Philadelphia: Fortress Press, 1983–85.

I. *Midrash in Context: Exegesis in Formative Judaism.* 1983.

II. *Messiah in Context: Israel's History and Destiny in Formative Judaism.* 1984.

III. *Torah: From Scroll to Symbol in Formative Judaism.* 1985.

FOUNDATIONS

OF JUDAISM

JACOB NEUSNER

FORTRESS PRESS   PHILADELPHIA

Library of Congress Cataloging-in-Publication Data

Neusner, Jacob, 1932–
   Foundations of Judaism.

   Abridged version of 3-part work published 1983–1985
under same title.
   Includes index.
   1. Judaism—Origin. 2. Judaism—History—Talmudic
period, 10–425. 3. Midrash—History and criticism.
4. Bible. O.T.—Criticism, interpretation, etc.,
Jewish. 5. Rabbinical literature—History and
criticism. 6. Messiah—History of doctrines.
7. Revelation (Jewish theology)—History of doctrines.
I. Title
BM601.N482   1988   296'.09'015   88–45246
ISBN 0–8006–2315–0

3460C88   Printed in the United States of America   1–2315

For

ADAM VAN DER WOUDE

University of Groningen

A token of appreciation to a good colleague
and a scholar of formidable standing and generous substance.

His research has always instructed me.
His collegiality has always won my heart.
His academic citizenship has always set the standard
to which others might aspire.

I am thankful to him for his many acts of
courtesy and respect,
and here express my appreciation for the man
and for his work of learning,
but above all,
for his setting the example of how scholarship in the humanities
may come to expression also in
profound and honorable humanity.

Contents

PART THREE: METHOD
TORAH, CANON, SAGE

Preface

From late antiquity to the present day, when people have referred to "Judaism" they have meant a very particular Judaic system, the one that (1) invokes as generative symbol the word Torah as sages, or "rabbis," represent the Torah, that (2) promises the coming of the Messiah when Israel, the Jewish people, observes the Torah as sages teach the Torah, and that (3) encompasses in the canon of the Torah revelation in two media, written (that is, the Hebrew Scriptures or "Old Testament" the world knows) and oral. The system as a whole forms a way of life—everyday actions, social existence—and a world view explaining that way of life and linking it to God's will for "Israel," defined as the children in a genealogical sense of Abraham, Isaac, and Jacob. In setting forth the foundations of Judaism, I spell out in the original context the principal contents of the Judaism of the dual Torah, written and oral. That Judaism emerged from a formative age of some six hundred years, from the first century to the seventh, and from the Jewish communities of the Land of Israel ("Palestine" or "the Holy Land") and Babylonia (present-day Iraq). It was in the fourth century, in the Land of Israel, in response to the triumph of Christianity in the Roman Empire, that the first outlines of that Judaism reached the same form in which we now know the system. So much for formative Judaism of a particular order: contents, context, time, place, circumstance. Now to the matter of foundations.

When I speak of "foundations," I mean two things that go together:

both (1) the beginnings and (2) the most important components. We want to know, concerning any great religious tradition, when and where and how things began, on the one side, and also the main points of the system, on the other. I believe that a clear and succinct picture of the foundations of Judaism will provide an example of how, out of diverse writings, we may describe any vast and complex religious tradition. For it seems to me that, in studying about any great religion, we should ask the same questions that we raise here: how does this religious tradition work, that is, how does it move from its holy books to its larger setting, from content to context; how does this religion explain its purposes and goals to its faithful; how does this religious tradition present, in a single vast and evocative symbol, the whole of its doctrine? By setting forth the Judaic system of the dual Torah within these categories, I hope to provide a useful example of describing a religious world out of its writings, an exercise in religious description. So I mean to address readers with a keen interest in religion (including, of course, both Jews and Christians).

That Judaic system described here took shape between the first and the fourth centuries of the Common Era (C.E.), and is represented by, in addition to the Hebrew Scriptures or "Old Testament," a variety of writings that, all together, present the contents of that other, oral Torah revealed by God to Moses at Sinai. In this book I outline the principal parts of the foundations of that Judaism of the dual Torah, specifically, the method, teleology, and doctrine of the Torah, or of Judaism as the great masters known as "our sages of blessed memory" taught that doctrine, spelled out that teleology in an everyday setting, and employed that method. The purpose of this book is to state clearly and succinctly the three basic elements of the system of the Judaism at hand as these take shape in the Judaic writings of late antiquity, from the Mishnah, the first document of Judaism after Scripture, brought to closure in ca. 200 C.E., through exegetical works serving the Mishnah, namely, the Tosefta, a collection of supplementary materials, the Talmud of the Land of Israel, ca. 400, and the Talmud of Babylonia, ca. 600; and through exegetical works, or commentaries, serving Scripture, specifically, to Genesis in Genesis Rabbah, to Exodus in Mekhilta, to Leviticus in Sifra and in Leviticus Rabbah, to Numbers in Sifré to Numbers, to Deuteronomy in Sifré to Deuteronomy, to the Five Scrolls (Ruth, Ecclesiastes/Qohelet, Song of Songs, Lamentations, and Esther), and some other writings. These works produced by "our sages of blessed memory" in late antiquity constitute the first stage in the unfolding, in writing, of the oral part of the one whole Torah of Moses, "our rabbi," and all together they form Judaism, that way of life and world view addressed to "all Israel" in the name of God speaking to Moses, "our rabbi," at Mount Sinai.

Let us now consider in some detail the canonical writings of the Judaism of the dual Torah. In this way the works cited in the present book will prove to be familiar and accessible, not simply an array of strange words referring to we know not what.

The documents of the formative period in the history of the Judaism at hand, the Judaism that rests on the premise that at Sinai God revealed the Torah in two media, written and oral, unfolded over a period of four hundred years or so. The first document beyond Scripture, the written Torah, was the Mishnah, represented later on as part of the oral Torah, which drew together teachings of authorities of the period beginning in the first century, before 70, when the Temple was destroyed and autonomous government ended, and ending with the publication of the Mishnah in ca. 200. The last of the documents of the oral Torah to reach written form in later antiquity was the Talmud of Babylonia (Bavli), which provided commentary on thirty-seven of the sixty-two tractates of the Mishnah as well as on substantial portions of the Hebrew Scriptures. In joining sustained discourse on the Scriptures, called, in the mythic of the present system, the written Torah, as well as on the Mishnah, held to be the oral, or memorized, Torah, the Bavli's framers presented a summa, an encyclopedia, of Judaism to guide Israel, the Jewish people, for many centuries to come. In between ca. 200, when autonomous government was well established again, and ca. 600, two types of books were written by sages who, under the authority in the Jewish governments recognized by Rome and Iran, held positions as political leaders of the Jewish communities of, respectively, the Land of Israel (to just after 400) and Babylonia (to about 500). One sort of books extended, amplified, systematized, and harmonized components of the legal system laid forth in the Mishnah. The work of Mishnah exegesis produced four principal documents as well as an apologia for the Mishnah.

This last—the rationale or apologia for the Mishnah—came first in time, about a generation or so beyond the publication of the Mishnah itself. It was tractate Abot, ca. 250 C.E., a collection of sayings attributed both to authorities whose names occur also in the Mishnah, and to some sages who flourished after the conclusion of the Mishnah. These later figures, who make no appearance in that document, stand at the end of the compilation. The other three continuators of the Mishnah were the Tosefta, the Talmud of the Land of Israel (the Yerushalmi), and the Bavli. The Tosefta, containing a small proportion of materials contemporaneous with those presently in the Mishnah and a very sizable proportion secondary to and dependent, even verbatim, on the Mishnah, reached conclusion some time after ca. 300 and before ca. 400. The Tosefta addresses the Mishnah; its name means "supplement," and its function was to supplement the rules of the original documents. The Yerushalmi mediates between the Tosefta and the Mishnah, commonly citing a paragraph of the Tosefta in juxtaposition with a paragraph of the Mishnah and commenting on both, or so arranging matters that the paragraph of the Tosefta serves, just as it should, to complement a paragraph of the Mishnah. The Bavli, following the Yerushalmi by about two centuries, pursues its own program, which, as was said, was to link the two Torahs and restate them as one. The Yerushalmi closed at ca. 400. The Bavli was completed by ca. 600. All these dates, of course, are rough guesses, but the sequence in which the documents made their appearance is not. The stream of exegesis of the Mishnah and exploration of its themes of law and philosophy flowed side by side with a second, much like the Mississippi and the Missouri where they meet at St. Louis and then flow side by side for miles beyond. This other river coursed up out of the deep wells of the written Scripture. But it surfaced only long after the work of Mishnah exegesis was well under way and followed the course of that exegesis, now extended to Scripture. The exegesis of the Hebrew Scriptures, a convention of all systems of Judaism from before the conclusion of Scripture itself, obviously occupied sages from the very origins of their group. No one began anywhere but in the encounter with the written Torah. But the writing down of exegeses of Scripture in a systematic way, signifying also the formulation of a program and a plan for the utilization of the written Torah in the unfolding literature of the Judaism taking shape in the centuries at hand, developed in a quite distinct circumstance.

Specifically, one aspect of the work of Mishnah exegesis began with one ineluctable question. How does a rule of the Mishnah relate to, or rest upon, a rule of Scripture? That question demanded an answer, so that the status of the Mishnah's rules and, right alongside, of the

Mishnah itself, could find a clear definition. Standing by itself, the Mishnah bore no explanation of why Israel should obey its rules and accept its vision. Brought into relationship to Scriptures, in mythic language, viewed as part of the Torah, the Mishnah gained access to the source of authority by definition operative in Israel, the Jewish people. Accordingly, the work of relating the Mishnah's rules to those of Scripture got under way alongside the formation of the Mishnah's rules themselves. Collecting and arranging exegeses of Scripture as these related to passages of the Mishnah first reached literary form in the Sifra, to Leviticus, and in two books, both called Sifré, one to Numbers, the other Deuteronomy. All three compositions accomplished much else. For, even at that early stage, exegeses of passages of Scripture in their own context and not only for the sake of Mishnah exegesis attracted attention. But a principal motif in all three books concerned the issue of Mishnah-Scripture relationships.

A second, still more fruitful path also emerged from the labor of Mishnah exegesis. As the work of Mishnah exegesis got under way, in the third century, exegetes of the Mishnah and others undertook a parallel labor. It was to work through verses of Scripture in exactly the same way—word for word, phrase for phrase, line for line—in which, to begin with, the exegetes of the Mishnah pursued the interpretation and explanation of the Mishnah. To state matters simply, precisely the types of exegesis that dictated the way in which sages read the Mishnah now guided their reading of Scripture as well. And, as people began to collect and organize comments in accord with the order of sentences and paragraphs of the Mishnah, they found the stimulation to collect and organize comments on clauses and verses of Scripture. As I said, this kind of work got under way in the Sifra and the two Sifrés. It reached massive and magnificent fulfillment in Genesis Rabbah, which, as its name tells us, presents a line-for-line reading of the Book of Genesis.

Beyond these two modes of exegesis and the organization of exegesis in books, first on the Mishnah, then on Scripture, lies yet a third. To understand it, we once more turn back to the Mishnah's great exegetes, represented to begin with in the Yerushalmi. While the original exegesis of the Mishnah in the Tosefta addressed the document under study through a line-by-line commentary, responding only in discrete and self-contained units of discourse, authors of units of discourse gathered in the next, the Yerushalmi, developed yet another mode of discourse entirely. They treated not phrases or sentences but principles and large-scale conceptual problems. They dealt not alone with a given topic, a subject and its rule, but with an encompassing problem, a principle and its implications for a number of topics and rules. This far more discursive and philosophical mode of thought produced for Mishnah exegesis, in somewhat smaller volume but in much richer contents, sustained essays on principles cutting across specific rules. And for Scripture, the work of sustained and broad-ranging discourse resulted in a second type of exegetical work, beyond that focused on words, phrases, and sentences.

Discursive exegesis is represented, to begin with, in Leviticus Rabbah, a document that reached closure, people generally suppose, sometime after Genesis Rabbah, thus in ca. 400–500, one might guess. Leviticus Rabbah presents not phrase-by-phrase systematic exegeses of verses in the Book of Leviticus, but a set of thirty-seven topical essays. These essays, syllogistic in purpose, take the form of citations and comments on verses of Scripture to be sure. But the compositions range widely over the far reaches of the Hebrew Scriptures while focusing narrowly upon a given theme. They moreover make quite distinctive points about that theme. Their essays constitute compositions, not merely composites. Whether devoted to God's favor to the poor and humble or to the dangers of drunkenness, the essays, exegetical in form, discursive in character, correspond to the equivalent, legal essays, amply represented in the Yerushalmi.

In this other mode of Scripture interpretation, too, the framers of the exegeses of Scripture accomplished in connection with Scripture what the Yerushalmi's exegetes of the Mishnah were doing in the same way at the same time. We move rapidly past yet a third mode of scriptural exegesis, one in which the order of Scripture's verses is left far behind, and in which topics, not passages of Scripture, take over as the mode of organizing thought. Represented by Pesiqta deR. Kahana, Lamentations Rabbati, and some other collections conventionally assigned to the sixth and seventh centuries, these entirely discursive compositions move out in their own direction, only marginally relating in mode of discourse to any counterpart types of composition in the Yerushalmi (or in the Bavli).

Through a rather circuitous path we return to the final document, the Bavli. This is where the two streams—Mishnah exegesis, Scripture exegesis—intermingled and flowed in one vast river. As I said at the outset, at the end of the extraordinary creative age of Judaism, the authors of units of discourse collected in the Bavli drew together the two, up-to-then distinct, modes of organizing thought, either around the Mishnah or around Scripture. They treated both Torahs, oral and written, as equally available in the work of organizing large-scale exercises of sustained inquiry. So we find in the Bavli a systematic treatment of some tractates of the Mishnah. And within the same aggregates of discourse, we also find (in somewhat smaller proportion to be sure, roughly 60 percent to roughly 40 percent in the sample I made of three tractates) a second principle of organizing and redaction. That principle dictates that ideas be laid out in line with verses of Scripture, themselves dealt with in cogent sequence, one by one, just as the Mishnah's sentences and paragraphs come under analysis, in cogent order and one by one.

We may well ask who speaks through these documents, so defining the community, authority, and authorship represented by them. The answer is critical to framing a valid perspective on the whole. But a brief answer nonetheless serves. The entire literature derives from only a single type of Israelite, a type represented in a single, continuous movement, with ongoing personal and institutional relationships beginning long before the closure of the Mishnah and continuing long after the conclusion of the Bavli. This movement—with its traditions of learning, its continuities of institutions, leadership, and authority, its assured social position and substantial political power in the government of Israel, the Jewish people, in both centers of settlement in late antiquity—bears several titles. It is called "rabbinic," because of the title of honor accorded to some of its leaders, called rabbis. But "rabbi" meant simply "my lord," thus, in context, not much more than "sir," or (*pro domo*) "professor." The term of honor occurs, with slight variation, in Christian Syriac sources, for example, Rabban, and therefore cannot connote a distinctively Jewish, let alone Judaic, meaning at all. Another title is "talmudic," because of the principal document, the Talmud (i.e., the Bavli, the Talmud of Babylonia) produced at the end. Hence people quite properly speak of "talmudic Judaism." Other, more theological titles circulate, for instance, "classical" or "normative," as in "classical Judaism" and "normative Judaism." Finally, within the system itself, the correct title would have to make use of the word "Torah," since the entire canonical literature forms "the one whole Torah of Moses, our rabbi," received from God at Mount Sinai. Accordingly, we could call the canon at hand the canon of the dual Torah, and the movement, the movement of Torah sages.

From our perspective a single fact emerges from the multiplicity of titles. The literature at hand derives from a singular group of intellectuals: well-organized sages. These sages also formed a political class within Israel in the Land of Israel and in Babylonia. They further served as models for the nation at large, models of not merely virtue but piety and holiness. So when we review what the literature of Judaism in its formative age has to tell us, from whom and what do we hear? We listen to that singular, distinctive vision that derives from men of intellect. And these facts further validate the hypothesis that the documents they produced exhibit important points of connection among themselves, as well as the proposal that the canon as a whole constitutes a classic case of intertextuality: writings that intersect broadly and deeply, that speak in a single way to a common conversation. The literary issue rests upon deep social and political foundations. And the foundations of Judaism therefore penetrate deep into the bedrock of the life of Israel, the Jewish people, from remote antiquity onward.

This book provides an abridgment of a three-volume study, as follows:

The Foundations of Judaism: Method, Teleology, Doctrine. Philadelphia: Fortress Press, 1983–85.

I.   *Midrash in Context: Exegesis in Formative Judaism.* 1983.
II.   *Messiah in Context: Israel's History and Destiny in Formative Judaism.* 1984.
III. *Torah: From Scroll to Symbol in Formative Judaism.* 1985.

I hope that by presenting the main results in a brief statement, I may make the matter accessible to a sizable audience of readers. My selections out of the original volumes are meant to be read on their own, but for full discussion and documentation, readers will want to take up the larger work. I have reorganized the order of topics, to conform to a logic of the whole to which the original volumes do not conform. Thus symbol here comes first, Messiah second, method ("Midrash") third. Passages from the Palestinian Talmud are from my translation, *The Talmud of the Land of Israel: A Preliminary Translation and Explanation* (Chicago: University of Chicago Press, 1982–), and employ the system of notation used there.

My thanks to Harold Rast, director of Fortress Press, for sharing my view that the three-volume statement of The Foundations of Judaism warranted an abbreviated expression, and, still more, for his warm appreciation and helpful criticism of everything I do. Working with Fortress Press draws me into a partnership with skilled professionals who, at the same time, bring to their work the common faith of the West in the God of Abraham, Isaac, Jacob—and Moses at Sinai.

JACOB NEUSNER

Program in Judaic Studies
Brown University
Providence, Rhode Island
July 28, 1988
My fifty-sixth birthday

TORAH AS SYMBOL

1

The Meaning of "Torah" in Judaism

Judaism as we know it at the end of late antiquity reached its now familiar definition when "the Torah" lost its capital letter and definite article and ultimately became "*torah*." What for nearly a millennium had been a particular scroll or book thus came to serve as a symbol of an entire system. When a rabbi spoke of *torah*, he no longer meant only a particular object, a scroll and its contents. Now he used the word to encompass a distinctive and well-defined world view and way of life. Torah now stood for something one does. Knowledge of the Torah promised not merely information about what people were supposed to do, but ultimate redemption or salvation. The shift in the use of the word, accomplished in a particular set of writings out of Judaism in late antiquity, appears dramatically in the following tale drawn from the last document to enter the canon, the Babylonian Talmud:

> R. Kahana [a disciple] went and hid under Rab's [his master's] bed. Hearing Rab "discoursing" and joking with his wife . . ., [Kahana] said to [Rab], "You would think that Abba's [Rab's] mouth had never before tasted the dish." [Rab] said to [Kahana], "Kahana, are you here? Get out! This is disgraceful!" [Kahana] replied, "My lord, it is a matter of *torah*, and I have the need to learn" (b. Ber. 62a).

As soon as we ask ourselves what the word *torah* means in such a context, we recognize the shift captured by the story. For—to state the obvious—to study "the Torah," meaning Scripture, one need not practice cultic voyeurism.

If, however, *torah* came to stand for something other than the particular writings comprising the ancient Israelite Scriptures, how do we trace the shift in content and usage? Clearly, the progress of the word and its meanings, both denotative and connotative, demands our attention. Within the expansion and revision of the word, originally referring to a set of books but in the end encompassing how one is to do even the most intimate deeds, we uncover the formative history of the Judaism for which the word Torah stands. That is the Judaism of the "one whole Torah," both written and oral, of "Moses, our rabbi"—Judaism as it has flourished from late antiquity to our own day.

When we take up the issue at hand, therefore, we confront the symbol that stands for the kind of Judaism presented by the Talmuds and related literature, defined by the authority of the rabbis who stand behind those documents, and best described as "the way of Torah." So far as outsiders supply the name of a religion, the one at hand may be called "rabbinic Judaism," or "talmudic Judaism," for its principal authority figure or authoritative document, or "normative Judaism," for the definitive theological status of the formulation at hand in the life of the Jewish people. But so far as insiders name the religion, that is, find language to capture and encompass the whole of what they do and believe, it is, as Kahana's statement tells us, "*torah*"—"and I have the need to learn."

The method is conventional and simple. I ask about the meanings various documents impute to a single word. I systematically classify and interpret the answers, so comparing one document to the next. The (more than occasionally) tedious task of consulting concordances for various rabbinical compositions and surveying the use of the word in documents lacking concordances yields facts that demand description and interpretation. The process of determining the meaning of a word in a given context requires little subjective evaluation but sustained objective elimination of impossible meanings. To give an example deriving from a front-page newspaper story, when we are told that "a brilliant filly" has died, we must ask what the adjective "brilliant" contributes to the noun "filly." Since a young mare can hardly have scored exceptionally high grades on an intelligence test, some other meaning must be implied. Along these same lines, we simply ask what a given noun can possibly mean in each distinct context, with the sole proviso that we take nothing for granted. That is, if we did not know what the word Torah would ultimately come to mean, in the full and rich sense imputed to it by the entire corpus of rabbinical writings at the end of their formative history, then what meaning should we uncover only in the particular passage at hand?

What "Torah" can mean, for example, in the mouth of Kahana, as he crawled out from under Rab's bed, is hardly self-evident. And how that word gained the entire burden of abstract meanings associated with it in the fullness of the kind of Judaism at hand is not yet known. The answers to these questions will provide us with the history of the principal doctrine of Judaism as we know it: all canonical writings of rabbis alike form statements of Torah. In the mythic formulation: "When God revealed Torah to Moses at Mount Sinai, God included the most recent and current convictions of authoritative living rabbis." Upon that myth—the Torah myth—rests the entirety of the system and structure of Judaism in its "classical," "rabbinical," "talmudic," "normative" formulation. The symbol of Torah defines Judaism as we know it. So, since the encompassing doctrine of Judaism is the doctrine of Torah, we trace the symbolic development of that doctrine.

2

From Scroll
to Symbol

A well-composed religious system will express in all of its details the main points of insistence of the whole. The sort of holy building people build, the sort of holy activity they deem worthwhile, the sort of consecrated family life they propagate, the sort of holy leader they envisage, the sort of holy community they form, and the sort of life beyond this life they promise—all express an essentially harmonious and cogent conviction. To state matters simply, everything repeats everything. Myth explains ritual. Ritual expresses myth. The histories of Judaisms—various religious systems, related to the same Scripture, produced by the people Israel, and intended to organize and make sense in supernatural categories of the historical life of that people—yield more than a few apt examples of well-composed religious systems.

One striking example derives from the Judaism of our own day. If we walk into any synagogue anywhere, our eye focuses upon what is in every synagogue the visual center: an ark containing a scroll, a Torah-scroll, a scroll containing the five books attributed to Moses. If we then ask what sort of activity the synagogue fosters, under all circumstances people speak of praying and studying the Torah, both activities falling within the same classification. If we inquire into who provides the leadership and how such a person qualifies, it is a rabbi, defined as one (usually male) who has mastered and now teaches the Torah. True, synagogue life consists of much more than classes of students who study the Torah. But the principal, and integrating, point of insistence stresses the act of studying a particular document in a particular way and doing what the rabbi says it ordains. Accordingly, Judaism as we know it presents itself to the world as the way of the Torah: studying the Torah and doing what the Torah commands.

Now when we turn back in time and ask about the origins of this Torah-centered form of Judaism, we move rapidly through the centuries from the twentieth through the nineteenth, eighteenth, and so on. All evidence from all places in which the people Israel has flourished yields essentially the same picture of Judaism. It was a religious system in which rabbis taught the Torah and governed the community in accordance with its theology and law. And yet, when we take account of what we know about the people Israel in ancient times, from its beginnings down to late antiquity, we realize that matters then were hardly as they have been for so many later centuries. When, for instance, we take up the sources of Judaism in the Near East in the ninth and tenth centuries, we find that "Torah" does not then stand for all the things it represents for most Jews later on. Controversy centered upon the canonicity of part of the Torah—the oral part, not written in the Pentateuch but gathered in the Talmuds and related literature. Accordingly, in our movement back through time, as we approach late antiquity, the world before Islam, we encounter the last stirrings of the struggle over the doctrine, hence also over the principal symbol, of Judaism that had earlier raged.

Moving rapidly over the formative centuries of Judaism as we know it, that is, the first seven centuries C.E., we reach a period before the age in which the Torah formed the principal symbol and visual center alike for a community of Jews. Indeed, we can identify a number of groups for which the Torah, while accepted as God's revelation to Moses at Sinai, competed with other modes of symbolization and other mythic messages entirely. Thus, were the Essenes whose library survived at Qumran to tell us what kind of building they would build for themselves, it surely would not take the form of a synagogue in town or village. We know that it took the form of a communal structure in the wilderness. In that building they studied Torah, to be sure. But their teacher was expected to do things rabbis rarely have been supposed to do. The life of the community followed paths that later Jews hardly explored. Again, during that phase of Christian history, in which Christianity formed a sector of the life of Israel, that group of Jews, while also revering the Torah as a mode of consecration, met around a table and ate cultic meals. To be sure, people taught the Torah. But the visual center, the expressive symbol, did not consist of a scroll; learning proved ancillary to other, more important acts, such as celibacy and martyrdom like that of Christ. A simple mental experiment, in which we asked diverse sorts of Jews in antiquity to tell us in a few words what they stood for, would yield a far broader range of symbolic systems than the Torah-centered one that has prevailed for so long. The result of that experiment defines the problem at hand. Let me spell it out.

The Torah of Moses clearly occupied a critical place in all systems of Judaism from the closure of the Torah-book, the Pentateuch, in the time of Ezra onward. But in late antiquity, for one group alone the book developed into an abstract and encompassing symbol, so that in the Judaism that took shape in the formative age, the first seven centuries C.E., everything was contained in that one thing. How so? When we speak of *torah*, in rabbinical literature of late antiquity, we no longer denote a particular book, on the one side, or the contents of such a book, on the other. Instead, we connote a broad range of clearly distinct categories of noun and verb, concrete fact and abstract relationship alike. "Torah" stands for a kind of human being. It connotes a social status and a sort of social group. It refers to a type of social relationship. It further denotes a legal status and differentiates among legal norms. As symbolic abstraction, the word encompasses things and persons, actions and status, points of social differentiation and legal and normative standing, as well as "revealed truth." In all, the main points of insistence of the whole of Israel's life and history come to full symbolic expression in that single word. If people wanted to explain how they would be saved, they would use the word Torah. If they wished to sort out their parlous relationships with Gentiles, they would use the word Torah. Torah stood for salvation and accounted for Israel's this-worldly condition and the hope, for both individual and nation alike, of life in the world to come. For the kind of Judaism under discussion, therefore, the word Torah stood for everything. The Torah symbolized the whole, at once and entire. When, therefore, we wish to describe the unfolding of the definitive doctrine of Judaism in its formative period, the first exercise consists in paying close attention to the meanings imputed to a single word.

To summarize the argument up to this point: The way of life and world view propagated by the Judaism represented by the principal documents of the formative age, the late second century through the seventh, stand alone in their focus upon the Torah. Other Judaisms, in which the Torah had its place as an element of divine service, built synagogues. The framers of the sort of Judaism at hand, called "rabbinic," from the honorific accorded its principal heroes, or "talmudic," from the title of its main literary record, or "classical" and "normative," by reference to the theological evaluation later accorded to it, built master-disciple Torah study circles. Others merely revered the Torah. The religious movement at hand took over the Torah and rewrote it in far broader terms than anyone else had ever imagined. Many kinds of Judaism believed in life after death and a world to come. But this distinctive sort of Judaism taught that, after death and in heaven, the Jews would study Torah under the direction of Moses and God. For ordinary Israelites, the biological father was the natural father and God in heaven the supernatural one. For this special sector of Israel, the master—the teacher, the rabbi—served as a supernatural father, taking priority over the this-worldly, natural one.

So, as is clear, every detail of the religious system at hand exhibits essentially the same point of insistence, captured in the simple notion of the Torah as the generative symbol, the total, exhaustive expression of the system as a whole. That is why the definitive ritual consisted in studying the Torah through the rites of discipleship. The definitive myth explained that one who studied Torah would become holy, like Moses, "our rabbi," and like God, in whose image humanity was made and whose Torah provided the plan and the model for what God wanted of a humanity created in his image. As Christians saw in Christ God made flesh, so the framers of the system of Judaism at hand found in the Torah that image of God to which Israel should aspire, and to which the sage in fact conformed.

In describing matters thus, I present a composite picture of how things were to emerge at the end of the formative age of the kind of Judaism under discussion. But we cannot take for granted that the way things came out at the end is how they always were. On the contrary, as soon as we recognized the novelty of the symbolic system of a Judaism expressed through new uses of the word Torah, the cultic activity of Torah-study, and the supernatural relationship of disciple to master of the Torah, we ask how it took shape. The system at hand, while absorbing much from its predecessors, was hardly congruent with anything that had gone before. Like earlier systems in some ways, unlike them in others, the talmudic-rabbinic-classical Judaism used the old in new ways and presented the whole fresh, an unprecedented system and structure.

Now to the range of meanings:

1. When the Torah refers to a particular thing, it is to a scroll containing divinely revealed words.
2. The Torah may further refer to revelation, not as an object but as a corpus of doctrine.
3. When one "does Torah," the disciple "studies" or "learns," and the master "teaches," Torah. Hence while the word Torah never appears as a verb, it does refer to an act.
4. The word also bears a quite separate sense, torah as category or classification or corpus of rules, e.g., "the torah of driving a car" is a usage entirely acceptable to some documents. This generic usage of the word does occur.
5. The word Torah very commonly refers to a status, distinct from and above another status, as "teachings of Torah" as against "teachings of scribes." For the two Talmuds that distinction is absolutely critical to the entire hermeneutic enterprise. But it is important even in the Mishnah.
6. Obviously, no account of the meaning of the word Torah can ignore the distinction between the two Torahs, written and oral. Hence I treat that as a distinct classification, even though it is important only in the secondary stages of the formation of the literature.
7. Finally, the word Torah refers to a source of salvation, often fully worked out in stories about how the individual and the nation will be saved through Torah. In general, the sense of the word "salvation" is not complicated. It is simply salvation in the way in which Deuteronomy and the Deuteronomic historians understand it: kings who do what God wants win battles, those who do not, lose. So too here, people who study and do Torah are saved from sickness and death, and the way Israel can save itself from its condition of degradation also is through Torah.

3

The Mishnah
and the Torah

When the authors of the Mishnah surveyed the landscape of Israel-ite writings down to their own time, they saw only Sinai, that is, what we now know as Scripture. Based on the documents they cite or mention, we can say with certainty that they knew the pentateuchal law. We may take for granted that they accepted as divine revelation also the Prophets and the Writings, to which they occasionally make reference. That they regarded as a single composition, that is, as revelation, *the Torah*, Prophets, and Writings appears from their references to the Torah, as a specific "book," and to a Torah-scroll. Accordingly, one important meaning associated with the word Torah, was concrete in the extreme. The Torah was a particular book or sets of books, regarded as holy, revealed to Moses at Sinai. That fact presents no surprise, since the Torah-scroll(s) had existed, it is gen-erally assumed, for many centuries before the closure of the Mishnah in 200 C.E.

What is surprising is that everything from the formation of the canon of the Torah to their own day seems to have proved null in their eyes. Between the Mishnah and Mount Sinai lay a vast, empty plain. From the perspective of the Torah myth as they must have known it, from Moses and the prophets, to before Judah the Patriarch, lay a great wasteland. So the concrete and physical meaning attach-ing to the word Torah, that is, *the Torah*, the Torah revealed by God to Moses at Mount Sinai (including the books of the Prophets and the Writings), bore a contrary implication. Beyond *The Torah* there was no *torah*. Besides the Pentateuch, Prophets, and Writings, not only did no physical scroll deserve veneration, but no corpus of writings demanded obedience. So the very limited sense in which the words *the Torah* were used passed a stern judgment upon everything else, all the other writings that we know circulated widely, in which other Jews alleged that God had spoken and said "these things."

The range of the excluded possibilities that other Jews explored demands no survey. It includes everything, not only the Gospels (by 200 C.E. long since in the hands of outsiders), but secret books, history books, psalms, wisdom writings, rejected works of prophecy—everything excluded from any biblical canon by whoever determined there should be a canon. If the library of the Essenes at Qumran tells us what might have been, then we must regard as remarkably impoverished the (imaginary) library that would have served the authors of the Mishnah: the Book of Books, but nothing else. We seldom see so stern, so austere a vision of what commands the status of holy revelation among Judaisms over time. The tastes of the Mishnah's authors express a kind of literary iconoclasm, but with a difference. The literary icons did survive in the churches of Christendom. But in their own society and sacred setting, the judgment of Mishnah's authors would prevail from its time to ours. Nothing in the Judaisms of the heritage from the Hebrew Scripture's time to the Mishnah's day would survive the implacable rejection of the framers of the Mishnah, unless under Christian auspices or buried in caves. So when we take up that first and simplest meaning associated with the word Torah, "*The* Torah," we confront a stunning judgment: this and nothing else, this alone, this thing alone of its kind and no other thing of similar kind.

We confront more than a closing off of old possibilities, ancient claims to the status of revelation. For, at the other end, out of *the Torah* as a particular thing, a collection of books, would emerge a new and remarkably varied set of meanings. Possibilities first generated by the fundamental meaning imputed to the word Torah would demand realization. How so? Once the choice for the denotative meaning of *the Torah* became canonical in the narrowest possible sense, the ranges of connotative meaning imputed to the Torah stretched forth to an endless horizon. So the one concrete meaning made possible many abstract ones, all related to that single starting point. Only at the end shall we clearly grasp, in a single tableau, the entire vista of possibilities. To begin with, it suffices to note that the Mishnah's theory of the Torah not only closed, but also opened, many paths.

4

The Theory of the
Torah in Tractate Abot

Approximately half a century after the closure of the Mishnah, a tractate containing sayings of authorities whose names occur in the Mishnah made its appearance. That tractate, Abot, the Fathers, begins with an explanation of the origins of the sayings of the authorities of the Mishnah. It therefore constitutes the first and most important apologetic for the Mishnah, explaining the authority of its authorities. The theory of the Torah presented in that important document emerges from the simple fact that what sages say in Abot begins at God's revelation of Torah to Moses at Sinai. We shall now see how that critical theory of authority in Judaism comes to concrete expression:

Abot
1:1–18

I. A. Moses received Torah at Sinai and handed it on to Joshua, Joshua to elders, and elders to prophets.
   B. And prophets handed it on to the Men of the Great Assembly.
   C. They said three things:
      (1) "Be prudent in judgment.
      (2) "Raise up many disciples.
      (3) "Make a fence for the Torah" [M. 1:1].
II. A. Simeon the Righteous was one of the last survivors of the great assembly.
    B. He would say: "On three things does the world stand:

          (1) "On the Torah,

          (2) "and on the Temple service,

          (3) "and on deeds of loving kindness" [M. 1:2].

III. A. Antigonos of Sokho received [the Torah] from Simeon the Righteous.

      B. He would say,

          (1) "Do not be like servants who serve the master on condition of receiving a reward,

          (2) "but [be] like servants who serve the master not on condition of receiving a reward.

          (3) "And let the fear of Heaven be upon you" [M. 1:3].

I. A. Yose b. Yoezer of Seredah and Yose b. Yohanan of Jerusalem received [it] from them.

      B. Yose b. Yoezer says,

          (1) "Let your house be a gathering place for sages.

          (2) "And wallow in the dust of their feet.

          (3) "And drink in their words with gusto" [M. 1:4].

      A. Yose b. Yohanan of Jerusalem says,

          (1) "Let your house be wide open.

          (2) "And seat the poor at your table

            ["make . . . members of your household"].

          (3) "And don't talk too much with women."

      B. (He spoke of a man's wife, all the more so is the rule to be applied to the wife of one's fellow. In this regard did sages say, "So long as a man talks too much with a woman, (1) he brings trouble on himself, (2) wastes time better spent on studying Torah, and (3) ends up an heir of Gehenna.") [M. 1:5].

II. A. Joshua b. Perahiah and Nittai the Arbelite received [it] from them.

      B. Joshua b. Perahiah says,

          (1) "Set up a master for yourself.

          (2) "And give yourself a fellow-disciple.

          (3) "And give everybody the benefit of the doubt" [M. 1:6].

      A. Nittai the Arbelite says,

          (1) "Keep away from a bad neighbor.

          (2) "And don't get involved with a bad man.

          (3) "And don't give up hope of retribution" [M. 1:7].

III. A. Judah b. Tabbai and Simeon b. Shatah received [it] from them.

      B. Judah b. Tabbai says,

          (1) "Don't make yourself like one of those who make advocacy before judges [while you yourself are judging a case].

          (2) "And when the litigants stand before you, regard them as guilty.

(3) "But when they leave you, regard them as acquitted, (when they have accepted your judgment)" [M. 1:8].

A. Simeon b. Shatah says

  (1) "Examine the witnesses with great care.

  (2) "And watch what you say,

  (3) "lest they learn from what you say how to lie" [M. 1:9].

IV. A. Shemaiah and Abtalion received [it] from them.

  B. Shemaiah says,

    (1) "Love work.

    (2) "Hate authority.

    (3) "Don't get friendly with the government" [M. 1:10].

  A. Abtalion says,

    (1) "Sages, watch what you say,

    "Lest you become liable to the punishment of exile, and go into exile to a place of bad water, and disciples who follow drink the bad water and die, and the name of Heaven be thereby profaned" [M. 1:11].

V. A. Hillel and Shammai received [it] from them.

  B. Hillel says,

    (1) "Be disciples of Aaron,

    (2) "loving peace and pursuing grace,

    (3) "loving people and drawing them near to the Torah" [M. 1:12].

  A. He would say [in Aramaic],

    (1) "A name made great is a name destroyed.

    (2) "And one who does not add subtracts.

    (3) "And who does not learn is liable to death.

    (4) "And the one who uses the crown passes away" [M. 1:13].

  A. He would say,

    (1) "If I am not for myself, who is for me?

    (2) "And when I am for myself, what am I?

    (3) "And if not now, when?" [M. 1:14]

  A. Shammai says,

    (1) "Make your learning of Torah a fixed obligation.

    (2) "Say little and do much.

    (3) "Greet everybody cheerfully" [M. 1:15].

I. A. Rabban Gamaliel says,

  (1) "Set up a master for yourself.

  (2) "Avoid doubt.

  (3) "Don't tithe by too much guesswork" [M. 1:16].

II. A. Simeon his son says,

  (1) "All my life I grew up among the sages, and I found nothing better for a person [the body] than silence.

(2) "And not the learning is the thing, but the doing.

(3) "And whoever talks too much causes sin" [M. 1:17].

III. A. Rabban Simeon b. Gamaliel says, "On three things does the world stand:

   (1) "on justice,

   (2) "on truth,

   (3) "and on peace,

   B. "as it is said, *Execute the judgment of truth and peace in your gates* (Zech. 8:16)" [M. 1:18].

The claim that Torah-study produces direct encounter with God forms part of Abot's thesis about the Torah. That claim, by itself, will hardly have surprised Israelite writers of wisdom books over a span of many centuries, whether those assembled in the Essene commune at Qumran, on the one side, or those represented in the pages of Proverbs and in many of the Psalms, or even the Deuteronomistic circle, on the other. A second glance at our tractate, however, produces a surprising fact. In Abot, Torah is instrumental. The figure of the sage, his ideals and conduct, forms the goal, focus and center. To state matters simply: Abot regards study of Torah as what a sage does. The substance of Torah is what a sage says. That is so whether or not the saying relates to scriptural revelation. The content of the sayings attributed to sages endows those sayings with self-validating status. The sages usually do not quote verses of Scripture and explain them, nor do they speak in God's name. Yet, it is clear, sages talk Torah. What follows? It is this: if a sage says something, what he says is Torah. More accurately, what he says falls into the classification of Torah. Accordingly, as I said, Abot treats Torah-learning as symptomatic, an indicator of the status of the sage, hence, as I said, as merely instrumental.

The simplest proof of that proposition lies in the recurrent formal structure of the document, the one thing the framers of the document never omit and always emphasize: (1) the *name* of the authority behind a saying, from Simeon the Righteous on downward, and (2) the connective-attributive "*says*." So what is important to the redactors is what they never have to tell us. Because a recognized sage makes a statement, what he says constitutes, in and of itself, a statement in the status of Torah.

To spell out what this means, let us look back at the opening sentences. Moses received Torah, and it reached the Men of the Great Assembly. The three things those men said bear no resemblance to anything we find in written Scripture. They focus upon the life of sagacity—prudence, discipleship, a fence around the Torah. And, as we proceed, we find time and again that, while the word Torah stands for two things, divine revelation and the act of study of divine revelation, it produces a single effect, the transformation of unformed man into sage.

When we review the classifications among which we earlier divided references to Torah in Abot, we find our catalogues merely perfunctory. In fact, in those taxa we miss the most important points of emphasis of the tractate. That is why, as I said, we have to locate the document's focus not on Torah but on the life of sagacity (including, to be sure, Torah-study). But what defines and delimits Torah? It is the sage himself. So we may simply state the tractate's definition of Torah: Torah is what a sage learns. Accordingly, the Mishnah contains Torah. It may well be thought to fall into the classification of Torah. But the reason, we recognize, is that authorities whose sayings are found in the Mishnah possess Torah from Sinai. What they say, we cannot overemphasize, is Torah. How do we know it? *It is a fact validated by the association of what they say with their own names.*

The instrumental status of the Torah, as well as of the Mishnah, lies in the net effect of their composition: the claim that through study of the Torah sages enter God's presence. So study of Torah serves a further goal, that of forming sages. The theory of Abot pertains to the religious standing and consequence of the learning of the sages. To be sure, a secondary effect of that theory endows with the status of revealed truth things sages say. But then, as I have stressed, it is because they say them, not because they have heard them in an endless chain back to Sinai. The fundament of truth is passed on through sagacity, not through already formulated and carefully memorized truths. That is why the single most important word in Abot also is the most common, the word "*says.*" At issue in Abot is not Torah, but the authority of the sage. It is that standing that transforms a saying into a Torah-saying, or to state matters more appropriately, that places a saying into the classification of Torah. Abot then stands as the first document of incipient rabbinism, that is, of the doctrine that the sage embodies the Torah and is a holy man, like Moses "our rabbi," in the likeness and image of God. The beginning is to claim that a saying falls into the category of Torah if a sage says it as Torah. The end will be to view the sage himself as Torah incarnate.

5

Meanings of "Torah" in the Yerushalmi

The Yerushalmi, or Talmud of the Land of Israel, presents us with the first full and complete statement of the principal meanings of the word "Torah" that the Judaism of the dual Torah would set forth. What is of critical importance in these meanings is simple. In the Yerushalmi the Mishnah's statements are referred to as "Torah." That is an enormous development, since it makes explicit the position implicit in tractate Abot, that the symbol of the Torah has acquired a sense unique to the Judaic system at hand. Once we reach, in describing a system, something unique, we realize that we have entered the heart of the system, that point at which everything is contained in one thing, at which the symbol becomes symbolic.

In the Yerushalmi a "word of Torah" may refer not only to the written Scriptures that everyone acknowledged, but also to the Mishnah. That presents enormously suggestive evidence of a shift in the meaning of the word Torah. In the following passage, the status of "Torah" is given to the words of the Mishnah. How so? Mishnah's statement serves as a proof-text as much as does the cited verse of Scripture[!]:

> Y. Sanhedrin 6:10:[III.A] R. Abbahu was bereaved. One of his children had passed away from him. R. Yohanan and R. Yose went up [to comfort him]. When they called on him, out of reverence for him, they did not utter to him a word of Torah. He said to them, "May the rabbis utter a word of Torah."

[B] They said to him, "Let our master teach us."

[C] He said to them, "Now if in regard to the [earthly] government below, in which there is no reliability, [but only] lying, deceit, favoritism, and bribe-taking—

[D] "which is here today and gone tomorrow—

[E] "if concerning that government, it is said, *And the relatives of the felon come and inquire after the welfare of the judges and of the witnesses, as if to say, 'We have nothing against you, for you judged honestly* (M. San. 6:10),'

[F] "in regard to the government above, in which there is reliability, no lying, deceit, favoritism, or bribe-taking—

[G] "and which endures forever and to all eternity—

[H] "all the more so are we obligated to accept upon ourselves the just decree [of that heavenly government]."

[I] And it says, *"That the Lord . . . may show you mercy, and have compassion on you . . ."* (Deut. 13:17).

The italicized words at E cite a passage of the Mishnah verbatim, while those at I use Scripture. Both provide proof of the same value, and, it follows, the Mishnah enjoys the status of Scripture and forms an equal part of the Torah. But in general, when the Talmud goes in search of proof-texts, it looks at revealed Scripture. That search for revelation testifies to a paramount—but no longer principal—meaning of the word Torah in the Talmud: revealed Scripture. To be sure, God may reveal his will through means not deemed Torah at all; an echo from heaven, for example (Y. Qid. 1:1), may declare the decided law. But the principal and authoritative source of revelation is Scripture.

Another important meaning of the word Torah, with roots in prior writings to be sure, is as an indicator of status. That is to say, something deriving from the Torah bears a higher status than what comes from sages' own reflection. What is most interesting in the Yerushalmi is that here the sage himself enjoys the status of the Torah.

Y. Sheqalim 5:1:[I.E] Said R. Eliezer, "It is written, 'This Ezra went up from Babylonia. He was a scribe skilled in the law of Moses which the Lord the God of Israel had given; and the king granted him all that he asked, for the hand of the Lord his God was upon him' (Ezra 7:6). Why does Scripture say, 'scribe'?

[F] "Just as he was a scribe for teachings of Torah, so he was a scribe for teachings of sages."

The master of Torah enjoys an independent position vis-à-vis the patriarch (Y. Hor. 3:1). How so? He instructs the patriarch in the Torah. When a master of Torah says a prayer, it is heard in heaven (Y. Hor. 3:4). People who honor sages will surely benefit. One gives precedence to his master over his father, the former enjoying a greater right of respect (Y. Hor. 3:4, 5). When a family attains merit through learning, it rises in formal status (Y. Hor. 3:5). An elder (sage) is of higher status than a prophet (Y. A.Z.2:7). When great sages die, the natural world takes note by exhibiting supernatural events (Y. A.Z.3:1). The sage enjoys a higher status than the patriarch (Y. A.Z.3:1). But the sage may well support himself through menial labor (Y. San. 2:6).

But these matters of social priority of the sage do not lead us to the heart of the matter. They reveal only the effects of a deeper conviction. The sage enjoys the high status accorded to him because he possesses and transmits Torah-sayings. That fact endows him with the status of the Torah—*and of the One who gave the Torah*. That claim to students of Judaism through the ages constitutes little more than a self-evident cliché. But in the literature that took shape before Yerushalmi, we do not find such a claim. And, as we are now coming to realize, the equation of Mishnah with Scripture, to which I alluded above, forms only one component in the nascent system as a whole. At hand is another, still more stunning element. The direct relationship between uttering a Torah-saying and God's revelation is made explicit in the following, which links one who utters such a saying to God:

> Y. Sanhedrin 10:1:[X.E] "Given by one shepherd"—(Qoh. 12:11).
> [F] Said the Holy One, blessed be He, "If you heard a teaching from an Israelite minor, and it gave pleasure to you, let it not be in your sight as if you heard it from a minor, but as if you heard it from an adult,
> [G] "and let it not be as if one heard it from an adult, but as if one heard it from a sage,
> [H] "and let it not be as if one heard it from a sage, but as if one heard it from a prophet,
> [I] "and let it not be as if one heard it from a prophet, but as if one heard it from the shepherd,
> [J] "and there is as a shepherd only Moses, in line with the following passage: 'Then he remembered the days of old, of Moses his servant. Where is he who brought up out of the sea the shepherds of his flock?

Where is he who put in the midst of them his holy Spirit? (Is. 63:11).
[K] "It is not as if one heard it from the shepherd but as if one heard it
from the Almighty."
[L] "Given by one Shepherd"—and there is only One who is the Holy
One, blessed be he, in line with that which you read in Scripture: "Hear,
O Israel: the Lord our God is one Lord" (Deut. 6:4).

The status of the sage is readily inferred from this passage. He is
placed on a continuum with God. The view is given below:

> Y. Sanhedrin 10:2[IV.H] So did Ahaz say, "If there are no lambs, there
> will be no sheep; if there are no sheep, there will be no flock; if there is
> no flock, there will be no shepherd; if there is no shepherd, there will be
> no world; if there is no world—as it were. . . ."
> [I] So did Ahaz reckon, saying, "If there are no children, there will be no
> adults; if there are no adults, there will be no sages; if there are no sages,
> there will be no prophets; if there are no prophets, there will be no Holy
> Spirit; if there is no Holy Spirit, there will be no synagogues or school-
> houses—as it were. . . . In that case, as it were, the Holy One, blessed be
> He, will not let his Presence rest upon Israel."

The upshot is that the master of Torah stands and speaks for God in
heaven. That is why the things he teaches—including Mishnah-tradi-
tions—enjoy the status of Torah. Accordingly, we claim too little
when we associate the word Torah only with the Mishnah, or only
with the Mishnah and succeeding documents. The word Torah first of
all served to establish a given status. What was equivalent to the
Torah became, itself, part of the Torah. Now, in the pages of the
Yerushalmi, we observe yet a third step, and a most important one.
The sage, the master of the Torah, now stands at the same exalted
level as does the Torah itself. The nascent conceptions of Abot come
to full realization in the tales we have just reviewed.

The Mishnah is held equivalent to Scripture (Y. Hor. 3:5). But the
Mishnah is not called Torah. Still, as I have pointed out, once the
Mishnah entered the status of Scripture, it would take but a short step
to a theory of the Mishnah as part of the revelation at Sinai—hence,
oral Torah. But sages recorded in this Talmud do not appear to have
taken that step.

In the Talmud at hand, we find the first glimmerings of an effort to
theorize in general, not merely in detail, about how specific teachings
of Mishnah relate to specific teachings of Scripture. The citing of

scriptural proof-texts for Mishnaic propositions, after all, would not have caused much surprise to the framers of the Mishnah; they themselves included such passages, though not often. But what conception of the Torah underlies such initiatives, and how do Yerushalmi sages propose to explain the phenomenon of the Mishnah as a whole? The following passage gives us one statement. It refers to the assertion at M. Hag. 1:8D that the laws on cultic cleanness presented in the Mishnah rest on deep and solid foundations in the Scripture.

> Y. Hagigah 1:7[V.A] *The laws of the Sabbath [M. 1:8B]:* R. Jonah said R. Hama bar Uqba raised the question [in reference to M. Hag. 1:8D's view that there are many verses of Scripture on cleanness], "And lo, it is written only, 'Nevertheless a spring or a cistern holding water shall be clean; but whatever touches their carcass shall be unclean' (Lev. 11:36). And from this verse you derive many laws. [So how can M. 1:8D say what it does about many verses for laws of cultic cleanness?]"
> [B] R. Zeira in the name of R. Yohanan: "If a law comes to hand and you do not know its nature, do not discard it for another one, for lo, many laws were started to Moses at Sinai, and all of them have been embedded in the Mishnah."

The truly striking assertion appears at B. The Mishnah now is claimed to contain statements made by God to Moses. Just how these statements found their way into the Mishnah, and which passages of the Mishnah contain them, we do not know. That is hardly important, given the fundamental assertion at hand. The passage proceeds to a further, and far more consequential, proposition. It asserts that part of the Torah was written down, and part was preserved in memory and transmitted orally. In context, moreover, that distinction must encompass the Mishnah, thus explaining its origin as part of the Torah. Here is a clear and unmistakable expression of the distinction between two forms in which a single Torah was revealed and handed on at Mount Sinai, part in writing, part orally. While the passage below does not make use of the language, *Torah*-in-writing and *Torah*-by-memory, it does refer to "the written" and "the oral." I believe myself fully justified in supplying the word Torah in square brackets. The reader will note, however, that the word Torah likewise does not occur at K, L. Only when the passage reaches its climax, at M, does it break down into a number of categories—Scripture, Mishnah, Talmud, laws, lore. It there makes the additional point that *everything* comes from Moses at Sinai. So the fully articulated theory of *two Torahs* (not merely one Torah in two forms) does not reach final expression in this passage. But short of explicit allusion to *Torah*-in-writing and *Torah*-by-memory, which (so far as I am able to discern) we find mainly in the Talmud of Babylonia, the ultimate theory of Torah of formative Judaism is at hand in what follows:

Y. Hagigah 1:7:[V.D] R. Zeirah in the name of R. Eleazar: "'Were I to write for him my laws by ten thousands, they would be regarded as a strange thing' (Hos. 8:12). Now is the greater part of the Torah written down? [Surely not. The oral part is much greater.] But more abundant are the matters which are derived by exegesis from the written [Torah] than those derived by exegesis from the oral [Torah]."

[E] And is that so?

[F] But more cherished are those matters which rest upon the written [Torah] than those which rest upon the oral [Torah].

[J] R. Haggai in the name of R. Samuel bar Nahman, "Some teachings were handed on orally, and some things were handed on in writing, and we do not know which of them is the more precious. But on the basis of that which is written, 'And the Lord said to Moses, Write these words; in accordance with these words I have made a covenant with you and with Israel' (Ex. 34:27), [we conclude] that the ones which are handed on orally are the more precious."

[K] R. Yohanan and R. Yudan b. R. Simeon—One said, "If you have kept what is preserved orally and also kept what is in writing, I shall make a covenant with you, and if not, I shall not make a covenant with you."

[L] The other said, "If you have kept what is preserved orally and you have kept what is preserved in writing, you shall receive a reward, and if not, you shall not receive a reward."

[M] [With reference to Deut. 9:10: "And on them was written according to all the words which the Lord spoke with you in the mount,"] said R. Joshua b. Levi, "He could have written, 'On them,' but wrote, 'And on them.' He could have written, 'All,' but wrote, 'According to all.' He could have written, 'Words,' but wrote, 'The words.' [These then serve as three encompassing clauses, serving to include] Scripture, Mishnah, Talmud, laws, and lore. Even what an experienced student in the future is going to teach before his master already has been stated to Moses at Sinai."

[N] What is the Scriptural basis for this view?

[O] "There is no remembrance of former things, nor will there be any remembrance of later things yet to happen among those who come after" (Qoh. 1:11).

[P] If someone says, "See, this is a new thing," his fellow will answer him, saying to him, "This has been around before us for a long time."

Here we have absolutely explicit evidence that people believed part of the Torah had been preserved not in writing but orally. Linking that part to the Mishnah remains a matter of implication. But it surely comes fairly close to the surface, when we are told that the Mishnah contains Torah-traditions revealed at Sinai. From that view it requires only a small step to the allegation that the Mishnah is part of the Torah, the oral part.

The Talmud of the Land of Israel presents us with a succinct and exhaustive description of what the Torah-way of life demands, as opposed to the requirements of any other mode of living. What is involved, quite simply, is perpetual concentration on teachings of the Torah and their performance, to the exclusion of other thoughts and deeds. Validation of that way of life, moreover, appears in the same context. It consists in the power to perform miracles, about which, in the next section, we shall hear a good deal more. The context requires attention, as we turn to the account of how one must act to conform to the Torah's mode of living. The important passage appears at F.

Y. Taanit 3:11:[IV.B] R. Adda bar Ahvah: When he wanted it to rain, he would merely take off his sandal [as a mark of the fast, and it would rain]. If he took off both of them, the world would overflow.
[C] There was a house that was about to collapse over there, and Rab set one of his disciples in the house, until they had cleared out everything from the house. When the disciple left the house, the house collapsed.
[D] And there are those who say that it was R. Adda bar Ahvah.
[E] Sages sent and said to him, "What sort of good deeds are to your credit [that you have that much merit]?"
[F] He said to them, "In my whole life no man ever got to the synagogue in the morning before I did. I never left anybody there when I went out. I never walked four cubits without speaking words of Torah. Nor did I ever mention teachings of Torah in an inappropriate setting. I never laid out a bed and slept for a regular period of time. I never took great strides among the associates. I never called a fellow by a nickname. I never rejoiced in the embarrassment of my fellow. I never cursed my fellow when I was lying by myself in bed. I never walked over in the marketplace to someone who owed me money.
[G] "In my entire life I never lost my temper in my household."
[H] This was meant to carry out that which is stated as follows: "I will

give heed to the way that is blameless. Oh when wilt thou come to me? I will walk with integrity of heart within my house" (Ps. 101:2).

We should err if we construed as essentially intellectual the ideal way of life subsumed under the word Torah. The issues are supernatural, the outcome is salvific (as I shall argue below). Adda bar Ahvah not only continually spoke words of Torah in appropriate places. He also behaved in a humble, self-controlled way. Yet at the center is the notion that a person continually repeats Torah-traditions and acts in accord with them. Accordingly, study of Torah involves more than acquiring information. It governs human relationships, specifically those between master and disciple.

But if people lived the Torah-way of life, then they had to find a balance between the demands of the world and the requirements of learning. They also had to know when one should set aside the processes of learning and undertake to perform what has been learned. The following story settles the question of whether or not to set aside Torah-learning for worldly benefit. The answer, of course, is that one must give up gain if it would interrupt study of Torah.

> Y. Sotah 9:13:[VI.A] *And faithful men came to an end.*
> [B] Said R. Zeira, "Men faithful to the Torah."
> [C] This is in line with the following: A certain rabbi would teach Scripture to his brother in Tyre, and when they came and called him to do business, he would say, "I am not going to take away from my fixed time to study. If the profit is going to come to me, let it come in due course [after my fixed time for study has ended]."

The definition of Torah as a way of life has focused our attention upon the supernatural issue: how learning in Torah transforms the learned man into a holy man. In the Talmud at hand, that issue comes to complete resolution. The holy man can do supernatural, that is to say, magical, deeds. So he can save himself and others from what threatens them, and, also, he can serve to save all Israel. We reach the definition, therefore, of a new category, one we have not discussed up to this point.

To define the category at hand, Torah as a source of salvation, I point to a story that explicitly states the proposition that the Torah constitutes a source of salvation. In this story we shall see that because people observed the rules of the Torah, they expected to be saved. And if they did not observe, they accepted their punishment. So the

Torah now stands for something more than revelation and a life of
study, and (it goes without saying) the sage now appears as a holy, not
merely a learned, man. This is because his knowledge of the Torah
has transformed him. Accordingly, we deal with a category of stories
and sayings about the Torah entirely different from what has gone
before.

> Y. Taanit 3:8:[II.A] As to Levi ben Sisi: troops came to his town. He
> took a scroll of the Torah and went up to the roof and said, "Lord of the
> ages! If a single word of this scroll of the Torah has been nullified [in our
> town], let them come up against us, and if not, let them go their way."
> [B] Forthwith people went looking for the troops but did not find them
> [because they had gone their way].
> [C] A disciple of his did the same thing, and his hand withered, but the
> troops went their way.
> [D] A disciple of his disciple did the same thing. His hand did not wither,
> but they also did not go their way.
> [E] This illustrates the following apophthegm: You can't insult an idiot,
> and dead skin does not feel the scalpel.

What is interesting here is how taxa into which the word Torah
previously fell have been absorbed and superseded in a new taxon.
The Torah is an object: "He took a scroll. . . . " It also constitutes God's
revelation to Israel: "If a single word. . . . " The outcome of the
revelation is to form an ongoing way of life, embodied in the sage
himself: "A disciple of his did the same thing. . . . " The sage plays an
intimate part in the supernatural event: "His hand withered. . . . "
Now can we categorize this story as a statement that the Torah
constitutes a particular object, or a source of divine revelation, or a
way of life? Yes and no. The Torah here stands not only for the things
we already have catalogued. It represents one more thing which takes
in all the others: Torah is a source of salvation. How so? The Torah
stands for, or constitutes, the way in which the people Israel saves
itself from marauders. This straightforward sense of salvation will not
have surprised the author of Deuteronomy.

This stunningly new usage of Torah found in the Talmud of the
Land of Israel emerges from a group of stories not readily classified in
our established categories. All of these stories treat the word Torah
(whether scroll, contents, or act of study) as source and guarantor of
salvation. Accordingly, evoking the word Torah forms the center-

piece of a theory of Israel's history, on the one side, and an account of the teleology of the entire system, on the other. Torah indeed has ceased to constitute a specific thing or even a category or classification when stories about studying the Torah yield not a judgment as to status (i.e., praise for the learned man) but promise for supernatural blessing now and salvation in time to come.

To the rabbis the principal salvific deed was to "study Torah," by which they meant memorizing Torah-sayings by constant repetition, and, as the Talmud itself amply testifies (for some sages) profound analytic inquiry into the meaning of those sayings. The innovation now is that this act of "study of Torah" imparts supernatural power of a material character. For example, by repeating words of Torah, the sage could ward off the angel of death and accomplish other kinds of miracles as well. So Torah-formulas served as incantations. Mastery of Torah transformed the man engaged in Torah-learning into a supernatural figure, who could do things ordinary folk could not do. The category of "Torah" had already vastly expanded so that through transformation of the Torah from a concrete thing to a symbol, a Torah-scroll could be compared to a man of Torah, namely, a rabbi. Now, once the principle had been established, that salvation would come from keeping God's will in general, as Israelite holy men had insisted for so many centuries, it was a small step for rabbis to identify their particular corpus of learning, namely, the Mishnah and associated sayings, with God's will expressed in Scripture, the universally acknowledged medium of revelation.

So the single most striking phenomenon, in the Talmuds and their associated exegetical compilations, now is the vastly expanded definition of the word Torah even in its symbolized form. It was deemed appropriate to invoke that symbol for a remarkable range of purposes. But the principal instance comes first, the claim that a sage (or, disciple of a sage) himself was equivalent to a scroll of the Torah. This constituted a material comparison, not merely a symbolic metaphor:

> Y. Moed Qatan 3:7:[X.A] He who sees a disciple of a sage who has died is as if he sees a scroll of the Torah that has been burned.
>
> Y. Moed Qatan 3:1:[XI.I] R. Jacob bar Abayye in the name of R. Aha: "An elder who forgot his learning because of some accident which happened to him—they treat him with the sanctity owing to an ark [of the Torah]."

What has happened here is that the sage finds his way into the center of the Torah, so that a single symbol—the Torah—now stands for the sage and his power, as much as for the Torah and its power. In this regard the rabbinic system finds its definitive characteristic, the identification of the sage with all of its symbolic structures, the attribution to the sage of every detail of the larger system's values. Not for nothing is the result, Judaism in its formative centuries, called "rabbinic." Indeed, as the word Torah moves from scroll to symbol, it joins a much broader movement still, always toward the sage.

It had been for a long time an axiom of all forms of Judaism that, because Israel had sinned, it was punished by being given over into the hands of earthly empires; when it atoned, it was, and again would be, removed from their power. The means of atonement, reconciliation with God, were specified elsewhere as study of Torah, practice of commandments, and performance of good deeds. Why so? The answer is distinctive to the matrix of our Talmud: When Jews in general had mastered Torah, they would become sages (rabbis), just as some had already become sages—saints and holy men of a particular sort. When all Jews became sages, they would no longer lie within the power of the nations, that is, of history. Then the Messiah would come. Redemption then depended upon all Israel's accepting the yoke of the Torah. Why so? Because at that point all Israel would attain a full and complete embodiment of Torah, revelation. Thus conforming to God's will and replicating heaven on earth, Israel, as a righteous, holy community of sages, would exercise the supernatural power of Torah. They would be able as a whole to accomplish what some few saintly rabbis now could do. With access to supernatural power, redemption would naturally follow.

The key to the Talmud's theory of the Torah therefore lies in its conception of the sage, to which that theory is subordinate. Once the sage reaches his full apotheosis as Torah incarnate, then, but only then, the Torah becomes (also) a source of salvation in the present concrete formulation of the matter. That is why we traced the doctrine of the Torah in the salvific process by elaborate citation of stories about sages, living Torahs, exercising the supernatural power of the Torah, and serving, like the Torah itself, to reveal God's will. Since the sage embodied the Torah and gave the Torah, the Torah naturally came to stand for the principal source of Israel's salvation, not merely a scroll, on the one side, or a source of revelation, on the other.

The history of the symbolization of the Torah proceeds from its removal from the framework of material objects, even from the limitations of its own contents, to its transformation into something quite different and abstract, quite distinct from the document and its teachings. The Torah stands for this something more, specifically, when it comes to be identified with a living person, the sage, and endowed with those particular traits that the sage claimed for himself. While we cannot say that the process of symbolization leading to the pure abstraction at hand moved in easy stages, we may still point to the stations that had to be passed in sequence. The word Torah reached the apologists for the Mishnah in its long-established meanings: Torah-scroll, contents of the Torah-scroll. But even in the Mishnah itself, these meanings provoked a secondary development, status of Torah as distinct from other (lower) status, hence, Torah-teaching in contradistinction to scribal-teaching. With that small and simple step, the Torah ceased to denote only a concrete and material thing— a scroll and its contents. It now connoted an abstract matter of status. And once made abstract, the symbol entered a secondary history beyond all limits imposed by the concrete object, including its specific teachings, the Torah-scroll.

I believe that Abot stands at the beginning of this process. In the history of the word Torah as abstract symbol, a metaphor serving to sort out one abstract status from another regained concrete and material reality of a new order entirely. For the message of Abot, as we saw, was that the Torah served the sage. How so? The Torah indicated who was a sage and who was not. Accordingly, the apology of Abot for the Mishnah was that the Mishnah contained things sages had said. What sages said formed a chain of tradition extending back to Sinai. Hence it was equivalent to the Torah. The upshot is that words of sages enjoyed the status of the Torah. The small step beyond, I think, was to claim that what sages said was Torah, *as much as what Scripture said was Torah*. And, a further small step (and the steps need not have been taken separately or in the order here suggested) moved matters to the position that there were two forms in which the Torah reached Israel: one [Torah] in writing, the other [Torah] handed on orally, that is, in memory. The final step, fully revealed in the Talmud at hand, brought the conception of Torah to its logical conclusion: what the sage said was in the status of the Torah, was Torah, because the sage was Torah incarnate. So the abstract symbol now became concrete and material once more. We recognize the many, diverse ways in which the Talmud stated that conviction. Every passage in which knowledge of the Torah yields power over this world and the next, capacity to coerce to the sage's will the natural and supernatural worlds alike, rests upon the same viewpoint.

The Talmud's theory of the Torah carries us through several stages in the processes of the symbolization of the word Torah. First transformed from something material and concrete into something abstract and beyond all metaphor, the word Torah finally emerged once more in a concrete aspect, now as the encompassing and universal mode of stating the whole doctrine, all at once, of Judaism in its formative age.

TORAH AND MESSIAH

6

Judaism a
Messianic Religion?

Since Judaism, represented by the symbol Torah, invariably is represented as a messianic religion, when we want to know the purpose and goal of the Judaic system of the dual Torah, we turn forthwith to the Messiah theme. In particular we ask whether Judaism as we know it constitutes a messianic religion, a religious tradition in which hope for a Messiah at the end of time frames the faith's world view and way of life. The question is critical because the heritage upon which Judaism in its rabbinic or talmudic form draws has nourished profoundly messianic offshoots (both Christianity and the Essene community at Qumran, for example). The kind of Judaism at hand, becoming normative later on, yielded one messianic movement after another. Given the character of the prophetic and apocalyptic literature of the Old Testament, we may hardly be surprised. So we wonder whether the formative canon of the kind of Judaism under study here both falls into the category of a messianic religion and also contains a systematic and well-formed doctrine worthy of an -ism, that is, a messianism. Does Judaism present a messianism, and may we therefore speak of the messianic idea or doctrine of Judaism?

The answer is a qualified negative, yielding a flat no. Judaism as we know it contains numerous allusions to a Messiah and references to what he will do. But so far as we examine the original canon of the ancient rabbis, framed over the second through seventh centuries, we find these inherited facts either reformed and reshaped for use in an essentially nonmessianic and ahistorical system, or left like rubble after a building has been completed: stones that might have been used, but were not. So Judaism as we know it presents no well-crafted doctrine of the Messiah, and thus its eschatology is framed within the methods of an essentially ahistorical teleology. Let me now spell out this thesis.

The Mishnah, which was the first document in the canon of formative Judaism, ca. 200 C.E., presented a system of Judaism aimed at the sanctification of Israel and bore a teleology lacking an eschatological dimension. From 400 to 600 the several successive documents of exegesis—the Talmud of the Land of Israel, the exegeses of scriptural books, and the Talmud of Babylonia—supplied the larger system of formative Judaism and rested upon the constitution of the Mishnah, with the well-established, eschatologically oriented teleology of the Messiah and his salvation that the Mishnah's framers had rejected. The Judaism that emerged was, and now remains, profoundly devoted to questions of history and its meaning and promised salvation through holy deeds of eschatological and salvific value. So the Mishnah, a system aimed at sanctification and built upon the main beams of nature and supernature, drew nearer to the orbit of the everyday life of Israel. The Talmuds and the collections of scriptural exegeses presented a system of Judaism focused upon salvation and which promised to carry Israel to the age that was to bring the Messiah and the end of history. Yet, as we shall see, the Messiah in the talmudic sector of the formative canon emerged as a figure meant to encourage and foster a view of life above time and beyond history, a life lived in full acceptance of God's rule in eternity, a life which rejected man's rule in history. The Mishnah had originally made that life the foundation of its system. Accordingly, when the canon of Judaism reached the end of its formative period, it presented a version of the Messiah myth entirely congruent with the character of the foundation document, the Mishnah. The Judaism emerging from late antiquity would then deliver to Israel an enduring message of timeless sanctification, in the guise of historical, and hence eschatological, salvation.

Here we trace two reciprocal processes: first, the "remessianization" of the canon of formative Judaism, and second, a re-formation of the Messiah myth to fit into the larger system expressed in that canon. In the end we shall be helped to grasp what is happening if we compare the Messiah in the canon of formative Judaism with the Messiah-myth development in the Christian understanding of Jesus as the

Christ. Early on, Christ the Messiah marked the end of history, the expectation of the imminent resurrection of the dead. Later on, the eschatological Messiah would become Jesus the rabbi, teacher, preacher, wonder-worker, God-man, perfect priest, and oblation. In other words the continuing life of the church turned Christ, the Messiah-Savior at the eschaton, into whatever Christians needed the Christ to be through the eternity of time. So the Messiah myth, originally defined in terms of antecedent Israelite conventions, entered the grid of Christian being, to be reframed and re-formed within that experience of the enduring "life in Christ." So too, in the formation of Judaism, was the eschatological Messiah (so critical to Paul's Christ) initially rejected as a category useful to the Mishnah's place in the canon. The Messiah myth would then regain pride of place within the Talmud's sector of the canon, but only in terms natural to the system inaugurated and defined by the Mishnah. Established conventions, whatever they were, would give way. The Messiah would serve Israel precisely as Israel's rabbis directed and would serve the Christian church just as the Christians wished.

In framing the issues in this way, I have used conventional understandings and categories. That is to say, I have worded matters as if there were such a thing as "the Messiah myth" which was connected with the resurrection of the dead, the rebuilding of the Temple, the last judgment, and various other familiar matters. These details derive from a well-known composite of information, "the Messiah idea" in "Judaism." But just as there was no single "Judaism," so, I shall argue, shall we look in vain for "the Messiah myth." First, "myth" promises a story, but there is no story. Second, as I shall show in the following chapters, "the Messiah" is an all-but-blank screen onto which a given community would project its concerns. The words "Messiah myth" bear little meaning other than the established and conventional one, which is wrong. I frame my argument not against but for, not to tear down what I believe to be unrefined and dull conceptions but to construct nuanced ones.

7

The Mishnah's Doctrine
of the Messiah and of History

When the Temple of Jerusalem fell to the Babylonians in 586 B.C.E., Israelite thinkers turned to the writing of history to explain what had happened. From that time onward, with the composition of the Pentateuch and the historical books, Joshua, Judges, Samuel, and Kings, to teach the lessons of history, and of the prophetic and apocalyptic books to interpret and project those lessons into the future, Israel explained the purpose of its being by focusing upon the meaning of events. The critical issue then was salvation—from what? for what? by whom? In that context, the belief in a supernatural man, an anointed savior or Messiah, formed a natural complement to a system in which teleology took the form of eschatology. Israelites do their duty because of what is happening and of where events will lead. All things point to a foreordained end, presenting the task of interpreting the signs of the times. No wonder, then, that when the Temple of Jerusalem fell to the Romans in 70 C.E., established patterns of thinking guided writers of Judaic apocalypse to pay attention to the meaning of history. In that setting, Jesus, whom Paul had earlier grasped in an essentially ahistoric framework, now turned out, in the hands of the writers of the Gospels, to be Israel's Messiah. He was *the* Messiah at the end of time, savior and redeemer of Israel from its historical calamity, thus a historical-political figure, the king of the Jews.

The character of the Israelite Scriptures, with their emphasis upon historical narrative as a mode of theological explanation, leads us to expect Judaism to evolve as a deeply messianic religion. With all prescribed actions pointed toward the coming of the Messiah at the end of time, and all interest focused upon answering the historical-salvific questions ("how long?"), Judaism from late antiquity to the present day presents no surprises. Its liturgy evokes historical events to prefigure salvation; prayers of petition repeatedly turn to the speedy coming of the Messiah; and the experience of worship invariably leaves the devotee expectant and hopeful. Just as rabbinic (now normative) Judaism is a deeply messianic religion, secular extensions of Judaism have commonly proposed secularized versions of the focus upon history and have shown interest in the purpose and denouement of events. Teleology again appears as an eschatology embodied in messianic symbols.

Yet, for a brief moment, a vast and influential document presented a kind of Judaism in which history did not define the main framework by which the issue of teleology took a form other than the familiar eschatological one and in which historical events were absorbed, through their trivialization in taxonomic structures, into an ahistorical system. In the kind of Judaism in this document, messiahs played a part. But these "anointed men" had no historical role. They undertook a task quite different from that assigned to Jesus by the framers of the Gospels. They were merely a species of priest, falling into one classification rather than another.

That document is the Mishnah, from about 200 C.E.; it is a strange corpus of normative statements which we may, though with some difficulty, classify as a law code or a school book for philosophical jurists. The difficulty of classification derives from the document's contents, which deal with topics to which we are reluctant to assign the title "law." Composed in an age in which people (the Romans included) were making law codes, the Mishnah presents a systematic account of the life of Israel, the Jewish people in the Land of Israel. The Mishnah comprises sixty-three tractates covering six categories of activity. These begin, first, with rules for the conduct of the economy (that is, agriculture) with special attention given to the farmers' provision of priestly rations. In the second are rules for various special holy days and seasons, especially for conducting the sacrificial service and life of the Temple cult on such occasions, and for the corresponding life in the home. Third are rules governing the status of women, with particular interest in the transfer of a woman from the domain of one man to that of another. Fourth is a code of civil laws, covering all

aspects of commercial, civil, and criminal law, and offering a blue-
print for an Israelite government based on the Temple in Jerusalem
and headed by a king and a high priest. Fifth, we find rules for the
Temple's sacrificial service and for the upkeep of the Temple buildings and establishment, with emphasis upon the life of the cult on
ordinary days. Finally, in the sixth category the Mishnah details
taboos affecting the cultic life in the form of unclean things and gives
rules on how to remove their effects.

This brief account of the document points toward its principal
point of interest: sanctification. At issue is holiness in the life of Israel
as it is lived out in relationship to the Temple and under the gov-
ernance of the priesthood. What has been said indicates also what the
document neglects to treat: salvation, that is, the historical life of the
Jewish nation, where it is heading, and how it will get there. The
Mishnah omits all reference to its own point of origin, and thus lacks a
historical account or a mythic base. The framers of the code likewise
barely refer to Scripture, rarely produce proof texts for their own
propositions, and never imitate ancient Hebraic modes of speech, as
do the writers of the Dead Sea Scrolls at Qumran. They hardly even
explain the relationship between their book and the established holy
Scriptures of Israel. As we shall see, the absence of sustained attention
to events or to a doctrine of history serves also to explain why the
Messiah as an eschatological figure makes no appearance in the system of the Mishnah.

Accordingly, the later decades of the second century, after the
defeat of Bar Kokhba, witnessed the composition of a vast book, the
Mishnah, which was later received as authoritative and turned into
the foundations of the two Talmuds—one composed in Babylonia, the
other in the Land of Israel—which define Judaism as we know it. If,
then, we ask about the original context of this foundation document
of the rabbinic canon, we find ourselves in an age that had witnessed
yet another messianic war, this one fought by Israel against Rome
under Bar Kokhba's leadership from 132 to 135. That war, coming
three generations after the destruction of the Temple, aimed to
regain Jerusalem in order to rebuild the Temple. It seems probable
that Bar Kokhba in his own day was perceived as a messianic general
and that the war was seen as coming at the expected end of time, the
eschatological climax to the drama begun in 70. If so, the character of
the Mishnah, the work of the war's survivors, proves truly astonishing.

Here, as I said, we have an immense, systematic, and encompassing picture of the life of Israel, in which events scarcely play a role. History never intervenes. The goal and purpose of it all find full and ample expression with scarcely a word about either the end of time or the coming of the Messiah. In a word, the Mishnah presents us with a kind of Judaism that has an eschatology without the Messiah, a teleology beyond time. When, in the Mishnah, the point of insistence is sanctification and not salvation, we see the outcome.

In what follows, I provide an account of how history is absorbed and reframed into an ontological structure. Here, specifically, is how history figures in the fantasy of a world beyond time, a world constructed in the minds of the Mishnah's sages. Survivors of the messianic cataclysm and catastrophe begun in the war of 66–73 and concluded in that of 132–35, they confronted in a fresh way the issues of Israelite existence as worked out by others through messianism. With the Temple site plowed over and Jerusalem closed to Jews, these sages created an imaginary city to replace the forbidden one; it was a detailed prescription for a cult to be taken in mind and studied in fantasy—a world contrived in the intellect.

So this great document, created by survivors and their disciples, contains a rich stash of question marks. Its authors tell us nothing about a theological context: the character and authority of the document, why they have made it, or what they want people to do with it. They ignore the entire antecedent literary heritage of Israel, referring only occasionally to Scripture but never to any other writing. The generative issues persistently addressed throughout the Mishnah's discourse concern sorting out matters of doubt, plotting the way in which conflicts between valid principles are resolved, and, in all, examining the way in which things reach their proper classification. These deeply philosophical questions take up problems of potentiality and actuality, intention and deed, the genus and the species, mixtures of various kinds, and similar perennial issues of thought. Inquiry comes to full exposure in discussions of arcane topics, most of them rarely, if ever, addressed in previous Israelite writings, except, in varying measure, in Scripture itself.

Accordingly, for all Judaism prior to its day, the document in context was unique. It adopted a position of splendid isolation from nearly all that had intervened from the closure of the scriptural writings to the formation of the Mishnah itself. The authors of the

Mishnah obviously drew upon facts available from their context, both contemporary and historical. But even here they pretended that Scripture was the sole source of facts. Where they assumed matters of fact that were not found in Scripture and sometimes even contradictory to Scripture, they silently passed over the issue of how they knew what they knew. They never squared what Scripture said, or did not say, with what they knew.

It was Judah the Patriarch (ca. 180–230), recognized by the Roman government as head of the Jewish community of the Land of Israel, who defined the standing of the Mishnah. Apparently he sponsored the document as the law code of the Jewish administration. Consequently, whatever the original intent of the framers—which we may guess only by induction from the things they did and did not do—the Mishnah, together with Scripture, rapidly became the constitution and bylaws of the Jewish nation in its Land. The clerks of Judah's government, who served also as judges in the petty claims courts governing the Jewish sector of the Land's mixed population, took over the Mishnah. They studied in laws, applied those that were relevant to their immediate task, and over a period of two hundred years developed a rather substantial corpus of mishnaic exegesis. That corpus, organized around specific clauses or paragraphs of the vast Mishnah, reaches us as the Talmud of the Land of Israel, brought to closure in the late fourth and early fifth centuries. The second Talmud, produced in Babylonia by the exilarch's clerks (counterparts of the patriarch's bureaucrats), reached closure probably a century and a half later. When, therefore, we approach the Mishnah, we take a path laid out for us by people who read the Mishnah with a particular purpose in mind. They transformed it into a document serviceable in courts and government bureaus. It became the original document, after Scripture, in the canon of formative Judaism.

If, for the moment, we turn back to the Mishnah of the beginning, as it stood before it took its large and commanding position over the life of Israel, the Jewish people, we survey the world as perceived by the Mishnah's framers, philosophical lawyers of the late second century. To be sure, as I said, they made ample use of whatever they chose to utilize out of the antecedent heritage of Israel. But it is their vision of how things should be framed and phrased that testifies to the original perspective. They laid the foundations. They selected the topics and arranged them. They determined the mode of thought (polythetic taxonomy) and the paramount method of discourse (list-making). They defined the logic and decided the system's distinctive structure and definitive traits.

To be sure, as I have explained, their successors in the Talmuds almost immediately rejected the system constructed by the sages of the second century. The heirs took whatever they found necessary, using the parts to make a different whole. The Talmuds' reading of the Mishnah consequently produced something quite different from what the framers of the Mishnah had anticipated. The talmudic system rested on foundations in the Mishnah, but proved to be radically asymmetrical to the Mishnah's own foundation. To state matters simply, by ca. 600 C.E. a system of Judaism emerged in which the Mishnah as foundation document would be asked to support a structure at best continuous with, but in no way fully defined by the outlines of, the Mishnah itself. The rabbi at the end was not the rabbi at the outset, and neither was his Torah, that is, his Judaism. The rabbi at the end saw himself as bearer and authority of the Mishnah, now legitimated as one half of the entire Torah of Moses, whom they called "our rabbi" and to whom they attributed the origin and foundation of the whole. So from whatever it was—perhaps a kind of remarkably arcane way of doing philosophy—the Mishnah became *torah* (revelation) and thus formed part of *the* Torah, the "one, whole" Torah revealed by God to Moses, "our rabbi," at Sinai. Hence, after Scripture itself, the Mishnah was the beginning of it all.

That is why, coming at the system from the endpoint, we ask the Mishnah to answer the questions at hand. What of the Messiah? When will he come? To whom, in Israel, will he come? And what must, or can, we do while we wait to hasten his coming? If we now reframe these questions and divest them of their mythic cloak, we ask about the Mishnah's theory of the history and destiny of Israel and the purpose of the Mishnah's own system in relationship to Israel's present and end: the implicit teleology of the philosophical law at hand.

Answering these questions out of the resources of the Mishnah is not possible. The Mishnah presents no large view of history. It contains no reflection whatever on the nature and meaning of the destruction of the Temple in 70 C.E., an event which surfaces only in connection with some changes in the law explained as resulting from the end of the cult. The Mishnah pays no attention to the matter of the end time. The word "salvation" is rare, "sanctification" commonplace. More strikingly, the framers of the Mishnah are virtually silent on the teleology of the system; they never tell us why we should do what the Mishnah tells us, let alone explain what will happen if we do. Incidents in the Mishnah are preserved either as narrative settings for the statement of the law, or, occasionally, as precedents. Historical events are classified and turned into entries on lists. But incidents in any case come few and far between. True, events do make an impact. But it always is for the Mishnah's own purpose and within its own taxonomic system and rule-seeking mode of thought. To be sure, the framers of the Mishnah may also have had a theory of the Messiah and of the meaning of Israel's history and destiny. But they kept it hidden, and their document manages to provide an immense account of Israel's life without explicitly telling us about such matters. To what may be implicit I confess myself blind and deaf: I see and hear only thin echoes of a timeless eternity governed by orderly rules.

When we walk the frontiers laid out by the Mishnah, we turn inward to gaze upon a portrait of the world at rest, in which, as I said, events take place, but history does not. It is a world of things in the right place, each with its proper name, all in the appropriate classification. In the Mishnah's world, all things aim at stasis both in nature and in society, with emphasis upon proper order and correct form. As we saw, the world of the Mishnah in large part encompasses the cult, the priesthood, and protection of the cult from sources of danger and uncleanness. The Mishnah presents a priestly conception of the world and creates a system aimed at the sanctification of Israel under the rule of the priests as a holy people. The world subject to discussion encompasses a temple, whose rules are carefully studied; a high priest, whose actions are meticulously chronicled; and a realm of the clean and the holy, whose taboos are spelled out in exquisite detail.

But, since none of these things existed when the framers of the Mishnah wrote about them, the Mishnah turns out to be something other than what it appears. It purports to describe how things are. But it tells us much more about a fantasy than about the real, palpable world, the world concretely known to the people who wrote about it. So the Mishnah is a work of imagination—using bits and pieces of facts, to be sure—made up in the minds of the framers of the Mishnah. The Mishnah does not undertake a description of a real building out there, maintained by real flesh-and-blood people, burning up kidneys of real lambs whose smoke you can smell and see. It is all a realm of made-up memories, artificial dreams, hopes, and yearnings. When we turn from the inner perspective to the sheltering world beyond, we see how totally fantastic was the fantasy. For the Mishnah provides prescriptions for preserving a world of stable order. Living in the aftermath of Bar Kokhba's defeat, the framers of the Mishnah in fact carried on through chaos and crisis, paying the psychic, as much as the political, costs of catastrophic defeat.

Lacking a temple or credible hope for one for the first time in Israelite history in the millennium from the rule of David onward, the sages confronted an Israel without blood rites to atone for sin and win God's favor. Under such circumstances, their minds might well have turned back to the time of David, and therefore forward to the age in which David's heir and successor would come to restore the Temple and rule Israel as God's anointed. Perhaps they did. Maybe in writing the Mishnah, they meant to describe how David's son would do things just as David had done things long ago. But if that was their purpose, they did not say so. And the one thing any student of the Mishnah knows is that its framers are pitiless in giving detail, in saying everything they wish, and in holding back—so far as we can tell—nothing we might need to know to plumb their meaning.

Yet we do not have to argue from their silence to find out what was in their minds. True, they speak little of the Messiah and rarely refer to events perceived as history. But they do record the events of the day when it serves their purposes. They do hint at the Messiah's coming. So let us rapidly survey some facts, rather than harping on the absence of evidence. If, for example, they give us no doctrine of the Messiah, no stories about him, no account of where he will come from, or how we shall know him, and what he will do, still, they do use the word "Messiah." How do they use it?

In a legal context, the Mishnah's framers know the anointing of a leader in connection with two officials: the high priest consecrated with oil, in contrast to the one consecrated merely by receiving the additional garments that indicate the office of high priest (M. Mak. 2:6; M. Meg. 1:9; M. Hor. 3:4), and the (high) priest anointed for the purpose of leading the army in war (M. Sot. 7:2; 8:1; M. Mak. 2:6). When the Mishnah uses the word Messiah in legal contexts the assumed meaning is always the anointed priest (M. Hor. 2:2, 3, 7; 3:4, 5).

Yet the Mishnah's framers know a quite separate referent for the same term. When they wish to distinguish between this age and the world to come, they speak (M. Ber. 1:5) of "this world and the days of the Messiah." That Messiah can only be the anointed savior of Israel. The reference is casual, the language routine, the purpose merely factual. Likewise, at M. Sot. 9:9–15 there is a reference to "the footsteps of the Messiah," again in the setting of the end of time and the age to come. That passage, a systematic eschatology, is critical for us in assessing whatever the Mishnah offers as a theory of Israel's history, so we shall review it in its entirety. (Biblical verses are cited in italics.)

M. SOTAH 9:9–15

9:9   I   A. When murderers became many, the rite of breaking the heifer's neck was canceled.

           B. [This was] when Eleazar b. Dinai came along, and he was also called Tehinah b. Perishah. Then they went and called him, "Son of a murderer."

    II   C. When adulterers became many, the ordeal of the bitter water was canceled.

           D. And Rabban Yohanan b. Zakkai canceled it, since it is said, *I will not punish your daughters when they commit whoredom, nor your daughters-in-law when they commit adultery, for they themselves go aside with whores* [Hos. 4:14].

    III   E. When Yose b. Yoezer of Seredah and Yose b. Yohanan of Jerusalem died, the grape clusters were canceled,

           F. since it is said, *There is no cluster to eat, my soul desires the first ripe fig* [Mic. 7:1].

9:10   A. Yohanan, high priest, did away with the confession concerning tithe.

           B. He also canceled the rite of the Awakeners and the Stunners.

           C. Until his time a hammer did strike in Jerusalem.

           D. And in his time no man had to ask concerning doubtfully tithed produce.

9:11 IV   A. When the Sanhedrin was canceled, singing at wedding feasts was canceled, since it is said, *They shall not drink wine with a song* [Isa. 24:9].

9:12 V   A. When the former prophets died out, the Urim and Tummim were canceled.

    VI   B. When the sanctuary was destroyed, the Shamir worm ceased and [so did] the honey of *supim*.

C. And faithful men came to an end,

D. since it is written, *Help, O Lord, for the godly man ceases* [Ps. 12:2].

E. Rabban Simeon b. Gamaliel says in the name of R. Joshua, "From the day the Temple was destroyed, there is no day on which there is no curse, and dew has not come down as a blessing. The good taste of produce is gone."

F. R. Yose says, "Also: the fatness of produce is gone."

9:13   A. R. Simeon b. Eleazar says, "[When] purity [ceased], it took away the taste and scent; [when] tithes [ceased], they took away the fatness of corn."

B. And sages say, "Fornication and witchcraft made an end to everything."

9:14 I   A. In the war against Vespasian they decreed against the wearing of wreaths by bridegrooms and against the wedding drum.

II   B. In the war against Titus they decreed against the wearing of wreaths by brides.

C. And [they decreed] that a man should not teach Greek to his son.

III.   D. In the last war [Bar Kokhba's] they decreed that a bride should not go out in a palanquin inside the town.

E. But our rabbis [thereafter] permitted the bride to go out in a palanquin inside the town.

9:15   A. When R. Meir died, makers of parables came to an end.

B. When Ben Azzai died, diligent students came to an end.

C. When Ben Zoma died, exegetes came to an end.

D. When R. Joshua died, goodness went away from the world.

E. When Rabban Simeon b. Gamaliel died, the locust came and troubles multiplied.

F. When R. Eleazar b. Azariah died, wealth went away from the sages.

G. When R. Aqiba died, the glory of the Torah came to an end.

H. When R. Hanina b. Dosa died, wonderworkers came to an end.

I. When R. Yose Qatnuta died, pietists went away.

J. (And why was he called "Qatnuta"? Because he was the least of the pietists.)

K. When Rabban Yohanan b. Zakkai died, the splendor of wisdom came to an end.

L. When Rabban Gamaliel the Elder died, the glory of the Torah came to an end, and cleanness and separateness perished.

M. When R. Ishmael b. Phiabi died, the splendor of the priesthood came to an end.

N. When Rabbi died, modesty and fear of sin came to an end.

O. R. Pinhas B. Yair says, "When the Temple was destroyed, associates became ashamed and so did free men, and they covered their heads.

P. "And wonderworkers became feeble. And violent men and big talkers grew strong.

Q. "And none expounds and none seeks [learning] and none asks.

I   R. "Upon whom shall we depend? Upon our Father in heaven."

S. R. Eliezer the Great says, "From the day on which the Temple was destroyed, sages began to be like scribes, and scribes like ministers, and ministers like ordinary folk.

T. "And the ordinary folk have become feeble.

U. "And none seeks.

V. "Upon whom shall we depend? Upon our Father in heaven."

W. With the footprints of the Messiah: presumption increases, and dearth increases.

X. The vine gives its fruit and wine at great cost.

Y. And the government turns to heresy.

Z. And there is no reproof.

AA. The gathering place will be for prostitution.

BB. And Galilee will be laid waste.

CC. And the Gablan will be made desolate.

DD. And the men of the frontier will go about from town to town, and none will take pity on them.

EE. And the wisdom of scribes will putrefy.

FF. And those who fear sin will be rejected.

GG. And the truth will be locked away.

HH. Children will shame elders, and elders will stand up before children.

II. *For the son dishonors the father and the daughter rises up against her mother, the daughter-in-law against her mother-in-law; a man's enemies are the men of his own house* [Mic. 7:6].

JJ. The face of the generation in the face of a dog.

KK. A son is not ashamed before his father.

III   LL. "Upon whom shall we depend? Upon our Father in
heaven."
        MM. Pinhas b. Yair says, "Heedfulness leads to [hygienic]
cleanliness, [hygienic] cleanliness leads to [cultic] cleanness, [cultic]
cleanness leads to abstinence, abstinence leads to holiness, holiness
leads to modesty, modesty leads to the fear of sin, the fear of sin
leads to piety, piety leads to the Holy Spirit, the Holy Spirit leads
to the resurrection of the dead, and the resurrection of the dead
comes through Elijah, blessed be his memory. Amen."

This is a long and rather complex construction. Concluding the
tractate, it is located after a legal passage on the topic of murder. I see
the following large, freestanding units: (1) M. Sot. 9:9–12, on the
gradual cessation of various rites, with an insertion at M. Sot. 9:10 and
an addition at M. Sot. 9:13; (2) M. Sot. 9:14, a triplet appropriately
inserted; (3) the melancholy list about how the deaths of various great
sages form a counterpart to the decline in the supernatural life of
Israel, M. 9:15A–N, presenting a rabbinic counterpart to the cultic
construction at the outset; (4) M. 9:15O–MM is diverse, but the main
beam—the phrase, "Upon whom shall we depend? Upon our Father
in heaven"—does appear. It appears to me that M. 9:15O–R form the
bridge, since the theme of the foregoing, the decline of the age
marked by the decay of the virtue associated with sages, is carried
forward, while the key phrase in what is to follow is introduced. W–
LL then go over the matter yet again.
        The Messiah, we notice, occurs rather incidentally and tangentially
at M. 9:15W. The important statement is at M. 9:15MM, where
Pinhas b. Yair accounts for the steps toward the end of time. The
important fact is that the Messiah does *not* mark off a rung. Instead
Pinhas lays emphasis upon personal virtues, the very virtues anyone
may master if he keeps the law of the Mishnah, with its interest in
particular in cultic cleanness, on the one side, and holiness on the
other. The virtue of each person governs the passage to the resurrection of the dead; everyone is supposed to be modest, fear sin, and
attain piety. All then are candidates, as potential sages, to receive the
Holy Spirit. If the Mishnah's pages contain a view of history and a
statement of the teleology of the law, it is in this brief statement of
Pinhas, and here alone.
        Elijah's insertion as herald of the resurrection of the dead, of

course, draws upon the well-known biblical allusion at Mal. 4:5, "Behold, I will send you Elijah the prophet before the great and terrible day of the Lord comes." The Mishnah's authors refer to Elijah as the forerunner of the end at M. Sheq. 2:5, M. B.M. 1:8, 2:8, 3:4–5. His task is to settle various disputed questions, in particular involving genealogy (M. Ed. 8:7). Allusion to Elijah here follows what again is a routine convention, established in Scripture, and in no way proposes a revision of it. For the philosophers of the Mishnah the Messiah figure presents no rich resource of myth or symbol. The Messiah forms part of the inherited, but essentially undifferentiated, background of factual materials. The figure is neither to be neglected nor to be exploited.

We therefore hardly find astonishing the failure of the Mishnah's lawyers to pay attention to the possibility of a false Messiah, nor do we even know what sort of Messiah would fall into that classification. The main concern expressed in the law on people who might mislead Israel focuses upon false prophets (M. San. 11:1B, 5) and blasphemers (M. San. 7:2). The principal concern is that people of this sort pose the danger of incitement to idolatry.

Accordingly, the figure of a Messiah at the end of time, coming to save Israel from whatever Israel needs to be saved, plays a negligible role in the Mishnah's discourse. It follows that fear of the wrong sort of Messiah likewise scarcely comes to the surface. Whether, at M. San. 7:2ff., idolatry or blasphemy in general served to encompass people who might falsely claim to inaugurate the end of time or to do the work of eschatological forgiveness of sins and the ultimate salvation of Israel, no one can say. It seems unlikely.

In all, the Messiah in the Mishnah does not stand at the forefront of the framers' consciousness. The issues encapsulated in the myth and person of the Messiah are scarcely addressed. The framers of the Mishnah do not resort to speculation about the Messiah as a historical-supernatural figure. So far as that kind of speculation provides the vehicle for reflection on salvific issues, or in mythic terms, narratives on the meaning of history and the destiny of Israel, we cannot say that the Mishnah's philosophers take up those encompassing categories of being: Where are we heading? What can we do about it? That does not mean questions found urgent in the aftermath of the destruction of the Temple and the disaster of Bar Kokhba failed to attract the attention of the Mishnah's sages. But they treated history in a different way, offering their own answers to its questions. To these we now turn.

By "history" I mean not merely events, but how events serve to teach lessons, reveal patterns, tell us what we must do and what will happen to us tomorrow. In that context, some events contain richer lessons than others; the destruction of the Temple of Jerusalem teaches more than a crop failure, being kidnapped into slavery more than stubbing one's toe. Furthermore, lessons taught by events— "history" in the didactic sense—follow a progression from trivial and private to consequential and public. The framers of the Mishnah explicitly refer to very few events, treating those they do mention with a focus quite separate from the unfolding events themselves. They rarely create narratives; historical events do not supply organizing categories or taxonomic classifications. We find no tractate devoted to the destruction of the Temple, no complete chapter detailing the events of Bar Kokhba nor even a sustained celebration of the events of the sages' own historical lives. When things that have happened are mentioned, it is neither to narrate nor to interpret and draw lessons from the events. It is either to illustrate a point of law or to pose a problem of the law—always *en passant*, never in a pointed way.

So when sages refer to what has happened, this is casual and tangential to the main discourse. For example, the "men slain at Tel Arza" (by the Romans?) come under discussion only because we have to decide whether they are to be declared legally dead so their wives may remarry (M. Yeb. 16:7). The advent of Gentiles to Jerusalem (in 70?) raises the question whether we assume a priest's wife has been raped (M. Ket. 2:9). A war begins—not named, not important—only because of a queen's vow, taken when her son goes off "to war" (M. Naz. 4:1). Famous events, such as the return to Zion from Babylonia in the time of Ezra and Nehemiah, gain entry into the Mishnah's discourse only because of the genealogical divisions of Israelite society into castes among the immigrants (M. Qid. 4:1). Where the Mishnah provides little tales or narratives, moreover, these more often treat how things in the cult are done in general than what, in particular, happened on some one day. For instance, there is the tale of the burning of the red cow (M. Par. chapter 3) or of the purification of the meṣora of Lev. 13:2ff. (M. Neg. chapter 14). The names of Temple officers are cataloged (M. Sheq. 51:1). But we learn no more about them than the jobs to which they were assigned. Allusions to famous events even within sages' own circles do not demand detailed narration (as at M. Kel. 5:10). It is sufficient to refer casually to well-known incidents. Narrative, in the Mishnah's limited rhetorical repertoire, is reserved for the narrow framework of what priests and others do on recurrent occasions and around the Temple. In all, that staple of history, stories about dramatic events and important deeds, provides little nourishment in the minds of the Mishnah's jurisprudents. Events, if they appear at all, are treated as trivial. They may be well known, but are consequential in some way other than is revealed in the detailed account of what actually happened.

The sages' treatment of events, as we shall now see in detail, determines what in the Mishnah is important *about* what happens. Since the greatest event in the century and a half (ca. 50 to ca. 200 C.E.) in which the Mishnah's materials came into being was the destruction of the Temple in 70, we must expect the Mishnah's treatment of that incident to illustrate the document's larger theory of history. The treatment of the destruction occurs in two ways.

First, the destruction of the Temple constitutes a noteworthy fact in the history of the law. Why? Because various laws about rite and cult had to undergo revision on account of the destruction. The following provides a stunningly apt example of how the Mishnah's philosophers regard what actually happened as being simply changes in the law:

M. ROSH HASHANAH 4:1–4

4:1 A. On the festival day of the New Year which coincided with the Sabbath,
B. in the Temple they would sound the *shofar.*
C. But not in the provinces.
D. When the Temple was destroyed, Rabban Yohanan ben Zakkai made the rule that they should sound the *shofar* in every locale in which there was a court.
E. Said R. Eleazar, "Rabban Yohanan b. Zakkai made that rule in the case of Yabneh alone."
F. They said to him, "All the same are Yabneh and every locale in which there is a court."

4:2 A. And in this regard also was Jerusalem ahead of Yabneh:
B. in every town which is within sight and sound [of Jerusalem], and nearby and able to come to Jerusalem, they sound the *shofar.*

C. But as to Yabneh, they sound the *shofar* only in the court alone.

4:3　A. In olden times the *lulab* was taken up in the Temple for seven days, and in the provinces for one day.

B. When the Temple was destroyed, Rabban Yohanan ben Zakkai made the rule that in the provinces the *lulab* should be taken up for seven days, as a memorial to the Temple;

C. and that the day [the sixteenth of Nisan] on which the *omer* is waved should be wholly prohibited [in regard to the eating of new produce] [M. Suk. 3:12].

4:4　A. At first they would receive testimony about the new moon all day long.

B. One time the witnesses came late, and the Levites consequently were mixed up as to [what] song [they should sing].

C. They made the rule that they should receive testimony [about the new moon] only up to the afternoon offering.

D. Then, if witnesses came after the afternoon offering, they would treat that entire day as holy, and the next day as holy too.

E. When the Temple was destroyed, Rabban Yohanan b. Zakkai made the rule that they should [once more] receive testimony about the new moon all day long.

F. Said R. Joshua b. Qorha, "This rule too did Rabban Yohanan b. Zakkai make:

G. "Even if the head of the court is located somewhere else, the witnesses should come only to the location of the council [to give testimony, and not to the location of the head of the court]."

The passages before us leave no doubt about what sages thought was important about the destruction: it produced changes in synagogue rites.

Second, although the sages surely mourned for the destruction and the loss of Israel's principal mode of worship, and certainly recorded the event of the ninth of Ab in the year 70 c.e., they did so in their characteristic way. They listed the event as an item in a catalog of things that are like one another and so demand the same response. But then the destruction no longer appears as a unique event. It is absorbed into a pattern of like disasters, all exhibiting similar taxonomic traits, events to which the people, now well-schooled in tragedy, well know the appropriate response. So it is in demonstrating regularity that sages reveal their way of coping. Then the uniqueness of the event fades away; its mundane character is emphasized. The power of taxonomy in imposing order upon chaos once more does its healing work. The consequence was the reassurance that historical events obeyed discoverable laws. Israel's ongoing life would override disruptive, one-time happenings. So catalogs of events, as much as lists of species of melons, served a brilliant apologetic by providing reassurance that nothing lies beyond the range and power of an ordering system and stabilizing pattern.

M: TAANIT 4:6–7

4:6 A. Five events took place for our fathers on the seventeenth of Tammuz, and five on the ninth of Ab.

B. On the seventeenth of Tammuz the tablets [or the Torah] were broken, the daily whole offering was canceled, the city wall was breached, Apostemos burned the Torah, and he set up an idol in the Temple.

C. On the ninth of Ab the decree was made against our forefathers that they should not enter the land, the first Temple was destroyed, then also the second, Betar was taken, and the city was plowed up [after the war of Hadrian].

D. When Ab comes, rejoicing diminishes.

4:7 A. In the week in which the ninth of Ab occurs it is prohibited to get a haircut and to wash one's clothes.

B. But on Thursday of that week these are permitted,

C. because of the honor due the Sabbath.

D. On the eve of the ninth of Ab a person should not eat two prepared dishes, nor should one eat meat or drink wine.

E. Rabban Simeon b. Gamaliel says, "He should make some change from ordinary procedures."

F. R. Judah declares people obligated to turn over beds.

G. But sages did not concur with him.

I include M. Taanit 4:7 to show the context of M. 4:6. The stunning calamities catalogued at M. 4:6 form groups, reveal common traits, and so are subject to classification. Then the laws of M. 4:7 provide regular rules for responding to and coping with these untimely catastrophes, all in a single classification. So the raw material of history is absorbed into the ahistorical, supernatural system of the Mishnah. The process of absorption and regularization of the unique and one-time moment is illustrated in the passage at hand.

Along these same lines, the entire history of the cult, so critical in the larger system created by the Mishnah's lawyers, produced a patterned, and therefore sensible and intelligible, picture. As is clear, everything that happened turned out to be susceptible of classification once the taxonomic traits were specified. A monothetic exercise, sorting out periods and their characteristics, took the place of narrative, to explain things in its own way: first this, then that, and, in consequence, the other. So in the neutral turf of holy ground, as much as in the trembling earth of the Temple mount, everything was absorbed into one thing, all classified in its proper place and by its appropriate rule. Indeed, so far as the lawyers proposed to write history at all, they wrote it into their picture of the long tale of the way in which Israel served God: the places in which the priests ate the meat left over for their portion after God's portion was set aside and burned up. This "historical" account forthwith generated precisely that problem of locating the regular and orderly, which the philosophers loved to investigate: the intersection of conflicting but equally correct taxonomic rules, as we see at M. Zeb. 14:9, below. The passage that follows therefore is history, so far as the Mishnah's creators proposed to write history, that is, to reduce events to rules forming compositions of regularity.

M. ZEBAHIM 14:4–9

14:4 I A. Before the tabernacle was set up, the high places were permitted, and [the sacrificial] service [was done by] the first born [Num. 3:12–13, 8:16–18].

B. When the tabernacle was set up, the high places were prohibited, and the [sacrificial] service [was done by] priests.

C. Most Holy Things were eaten within the veils; Lesser Holy Things [were eaten] throughout the camp of Israel.

14:5 II A. They came to Gilgal.

B. The high places were permitted.

C. Most Holy Things were eaten within the veils, Lesser Holy Things, anywhere.

14:6 III A. They came to Shiloh

B. The high places were prohibited.

C. There was no roof beam there, but below was a house of stone, and hangings above it, and it was *the resting place* [Deut. 12:9].

D. Most Holy Things were eaten within the veils, Lesser Holy Things and second tithe [were eaten] in any place within sight [of Shiloh].

14:7   IV   A. They came to Nob and Gibeon.
            B. The high places were permitted.
            C. Most Holy Things were eaten within the veils, Lesser
       Holy Things, in all the towns of Israel.
14:8   V   A. They came to Jerusalem.
            B. The high places were prohibited.
            C. And they never again were permitted.
            D. And it was *"the inheritance"* [Deut. 12:9].
            E. Most Holy Things were eaten within the veils, Lesser
       Holy Things and second tithe within the wall.
14:9   A. All the Holy Things which one sanctified at the time of
       the prohibition of the high places and offered at the time of the
       prohibition of high places outside—
            B. lo, these are subject to the transgression of a positive
       commandment and a negative commandment, and they are
       liable on their account to extirpation [for sacrificing outside the
       designated place, Lev. 17:8-9, M. Zeb. 13:1A].
            C. [If] one sanctified them at the time of the permission of
       high places and offered them up at the time of the prohibition of
       high places,
            D. lo, these are subject to transgression of a positive com-
       mandment and to a negative commandment, but they are not
       liable on their account to extirpation [since if the offerings had
       been sacrificed when they were sanctified, there should have
       been no violation].
            E. [If] one sanctified them at the time of the prohibition of
       high places and offered them up at the time of the permission of
       high places,
            F. lo, these are subject to transgression of a positive com-
       mandment, but they are not subject to a negative commandment
       at all.

The inclusion of M. Zeb. 14:9, structurally matching M. Ta. 4:7, shows
us the goal of the historical composition. It is to set forth rules that
intersect and produce confusion, so that we may sort out confusion
and make sense of all the data. To see M. Zeb. in context, we have to
return to the passage of M. Sot.

    History as a composition of successive, internally symmetrical pat-
terns provides one model for lawyers proposing to relate Israel's life in
time. A second historical picture has already passed before us, in
which sages propose a pattern of events, the one at M. Sot. 9:9-15.
What is striking in that passage is that, when sages define the patterns

of history, they scarcely speak about events—things that actually happen at some one time and bear deep meaning.

M. Sot. 9:15 expresses a view of history that we may represent as a V, a long downward progression followed by an upward ascent. The descent is marked, as we noticed, by the successive nullification of rites of the cult, by the disappearance of marks of supernatural favor to Israel. The destruction represents the climax, as well it should. At that point, the "faithful men" also come to an end. The cult's end then marks the beginning, also, of the loss of holy sages. These are not messiahs; their virtue is sagacity. The long path downward ends with the climactic assertion, three times, that Israel must depend upon the heavenly father. To this picture the Messiah is at best incidental. The upward side of the V is then traced in steps of priests' and sages' virtues, things people can do which at the end will lead to the Holy Spirit and the resurrection of the dead. To all of this, the Messiah is again incidental; the omission becomes striking when we learn that Elijah, not the Messiah, will restore the dead to life.

Now on the basis of this passage, we may posit the existence of a generally prevailing theory of the Messiah's coming. That theory was accepted by the framers of this passage. But they restated it in terms of what is particular and distinctive to their points of systemic insistence. Accordingly, we may surmise that Jews in general believed in the coming of a Messiah, and in the resurrection of the dead, which was somehow related to that advent. They further believed that the "footprints of the Messiah" would mark a path through deepening darkness and decay, a world so miserable that only supernatural intervention could save it. But in the Mishnah that conviction—a commonplace in Israel's life—is reworked in terms of the definitive values of the framers of the passage, the sages' group. In particular, in references to the wisdom of scribes and fear of sin, not to mention the absence of respect for elders and fathers so characteristic of this group, we see the marks of their distinctive set of values. To others it may have been a mere detail; to the framer of this passage it indicated the crux of the matter.

At issue in the end is the direction of eschatology in the foundation document and in its continuations. It is not merely whether, or how frequently, the figures of the Messiah and Elijah make an appearance, how often "the days of the Messiah" come under discussion, or how many references we find to "the end of days" or events we regard as historical. We focus upon how the system which was laid out in the Mishnah takes up and disposes of those critical issues of teleology which were worked out through messianic eschatology in other, earlier versions of Judaism. These earlier systems resorted to the myth of the Messiah as savior and redeemer of Israel, a supernatural figure engaged in political-historical tasks as king of the Jews, even a God-man facing the crucial historical questions of Israel's life and then resolving them—Christ as king of the world, of the ages, even of death itself. Although the figure of a Messiah does appear, when the framers of the Mishnah spoke of "the Messiah," they meant a high priest designated and consecrated to office in a certain way, and not in some other way. The reference to "days of the Messiah" constitutes a conventional division of history at the end time but before the ultimate end. But that category of time plays no consequential role in the teleological framework established within the Mishnah. Accordingly, the Mishnah's framers constructed a system of Judaism in which the entire teleological dimension reached full exposure while hardly invoking the person or functions of a messianic figure of any kind. Perhaps in the aftermath of Bar Kokhba's debacle, silence on the subject served to express a clarion judgment. I am inclined to think so. But, for the purpose of our inquiry, the main thing is a simple fact, now fully expounded and illustrated.

The issue of eschatology, framed in mythic terms, draws in its wake the issue of how, in the foundation document of Judaism, history comes to full conceptual expression. "History" as an account of a meaningful pattern of events, a making sense of the past and giving guidance about the future, begins with the necessary conviction that events matter, one after another. The Mishnah's framers present us with no elaborate theory of events, a fact fully consonant with their systematic points of insistence and encompassing concern. Events do not matter, not one by one.

The philosopher-lawyers exhibited no theory of history either. Their conception of Israel's destiny in no way called upon historical categories of either narrative or didactic explanation to describe and account for the future. The small importance attributed to the figure of the Messiah as a historical-eschatological figure, therefore, fully accords with the larger traits of the system as a whole. Let me speak with emphasis: *If what is important in Israel's existence were sanctification, an ongoing process, and not salvation, understood as a one-*

*time event at the end, then no one would find reason to narrate
history.* Few then would form the obsession about the Messiah so
characteristic of Judaism in its later, rabbinic mode. But, as we shall
see, the Messiah then would wear a rabbinical cloak and draw Israel
to accept the Talmud's irenic conception of the holy life. Salvation
comes through sanctification, just as M. Sot. 9:15 indicates. The salvific figure, then, becomes an instrument of consecration and so fits into
a system quite different from the one originally built around the
Messiah.

Judaism at the end did indeed provide an ample account and
explanation of Israel's history and destiny. These emerged as the
generative problem of Judaism, just as they framed the social reality
confronted by Jews wherever they lived. So, to seek the map that
shows the road from the Mishnah, at the beginning, to the fully
articulated Judaism at the end of the formative age in late antiquity,
we have to look elsewhere.

The critical issues confronting the Jewish nation emerged from its
sorry political condition. In the most commonplace sense of the word,
these were *historical* issues. Any sort of Judaism that pretended the
history of Israel could be reduced to lists of events sharing the same
taxonomic traits. That the destiny of Israel might be absorbed into an
essentially imaginary framework of sanctification attained through
the human heart and mind, demanded what the Jewish nation could
not give. For people could not pretend to be other than who they
were and what they were. Israel constituted a defeated people, driven
from its holy place, yet reminded, every time it opened its ancient
Scriptures, of God's special love for it and of its distinctive destiny
among nations. Israel lived out an insufferable paradox between
God's word and world, between promise and postponed fulfillment.
So the critical issue confronting any sort of Judaism to emerge in late
antiquity reached definition and attained urgency in the social reality, the everyday experience, of Israel: When? By whom? To the
Jewish nation history proved very real indeed. The political question
of Israel's destiny settled by the myth of the promise of the Messiah's
coming salvation—a concrete, national, and historical salvation—
could not be wished away. It demanded response: how long, O Lord?
So, as is clear, the Mishnah's system would have to undergo revision
and reformation. The labor of renewal would demand fresh and
original thinkers: exegetes of a remarkably subtle capacity.

8

The Messiah
and the Doctrine of
History in the Yerushalmi

The Talmud of the Land of Israel presents clear evidence that the Messiah myth had come into a process of absorption and assimilation within the larger Torah myth which was characteristic of Judaism in its formative and later literature. We find a clear effort to identify the person of the Messiah and to confront the claim that a specific, named individual had been, or would be, the Messiah. This means that the issue had reached the center of lively discourse at least in some rabbinic circles. Two contexts framed discussion, the destruction of the Temple and the messianic claim of Bar Kokhba.

As to the former, we find a statement that the Messiah was born on the day the Temple was destroyed. Accordingly, once the figure of the Messiah had come on stage, there arises discussion on who, among the living, the Messiah might be. The identification of the Messiah begins, of course, with the person of David himself: "If the Messiah-King comes from among the living, his name will be David. If he comes from among the dead, it will be King David himself." A variety of evidence announced the advent of the Messiah as a figure in the larger system of formative Judaism. The rabbinization of David constitutes one kind of evidence. Serious discussion, within the framework of the accepted document of mishnaic exegesis and the law, concerning the identification and claim of diverse figures asserted to be messiahs, presents still more telling proof.

Y. BERAKHOT 2:4
(TRANSLATED BY T. ZAHAVY)

[A] Once a Jew was plowing and his ox snorted once before him. An Arab who was passing and heard the sound said to him, "Jew, loosen your ox and loosen the plow and stop plowing. For today your Temple was destroyed."

[B] The ox snorted again. He [the Arab] said to him, "Jew, bind your ox and bind your plow, for today the Messiah-King was born."

[C] He said to him, "What is his name?"

[D] "Menahem."

[E] He said to him, "And what is his father's name?"

[F] The Arab said to him, "Hezekiah."

[G] He said to him, "Where is he from?"

[H] He said to him, "From the royal capital of Bethlehem in Judea."

[I] The Jew went and sold his ox and sold his plow. And he became a peddler of infant's felt-cloth [diapers]. And he went from place to place until he came to that very city. All of the women bought from him. But Menahem's mother did not buy from him.

[J] He heard the women saying, "Menahem's mother, Menahem's mother, come buy for your child."

[K] She said, "I want to bring him up to hate Israel. For on the day he was born, the Temple was destroyed."

[L] They said to her, "We are sure that on this day it was destroyed, and on this day of the year it will be rebuilt."

[M] She said to the peddler, "I have no money."

[N] He said to her, "It is of no matter to me. Come and buy for him and pay me when I return."

[O] A while later he returned to that city. He said to her, "How is the infant doing?"

[P] She said to him, "Since the time you saw him a spirit came and carried him away from me."

[Q] Said R. Bun, "Why do we learn this from [a story about] an Arab? Do we not have explicit scriptural evidence for it? *Lebanon with its majestic trees will fall* [Isa. 10:34]. And what follows this? *There shall come forth a shoot from the stump* of Jesse [Isa. 11:1]. [Right after an allusion to the destruction of the Temple the prophet speaks of the messianic age.]"

This is a set-piece story, adduced to prove that the Messiah was born on the day the Temple was destroyed. Its importance for our purpose is to indicate that elaborate materials on the Messiah—on his coming, his name, and the like—now found a comfortable place within the rabbinic canon. The contrast to the character of discourse in the Mishnah is stunning. From perfunctory allusions, we now move to powerful and suggestive tales. Whether the tale at hand was made up by rabbis to serve some larger systemic purpose is hardly clear. The Messiah was born when the Temple was destroyed; hence, God prepared for Israel a better fate than had appeared.

A more concrete matter—the identification of the Messiah with a known historical personality—was associated with the name of Aqiba. He is said to have claimed that Bar Kokhba, leader of the second-century revolt, was the Messiah. The important aspect of the story, however, is the rejection of Aqiba's view. The discredited messiah figure (if Bar Kokhba actually was such in his own day) finds no apologists in the later rabbinical canon. What is striking in what follows, moreover, is that we really have two stories. At G, Aqiba is said to have believed that Bar Kokhba was a disappointment. At H–I, he is said to have identified Bar Kokhba with the King-Messiah. Both cannot be true, so what we have is simply two separate opinions of Aqiba's judgment of Bar Kokhba/Bar Kozebah.

Y. TAANIT 4:5

[X G] R. Simeon b. Yohai taught, "Aqiba, my master, would interpret the following verse: '*A star (kokhab) shall come forth out of Jacob*' [Num. 24:17]. 'A disappointment (Kozeba) shall come forth out of Jacob.'"

[H] R. Aqiba, when he saw Bar Kozeba, said, "This is the King Messiah."
[I] R. Yohanan ben Toreta said to him, "Aqiba! Grass will grow on your cheeks before the Messiah will come!"

The important point is not only that Aqiba had been proved wrong. It is that the very verse of Scripture adduced in behalf of his viewpoint could be treated more generally and made to refer to righteous people in general, not to *the* Messiah in particular.

Y. NEDARIM 3:8

[I F] R. Gershom in the name of R. Aha: "'*[I see him, but not now; I behold him, but not nigh;] a star shall come out of Jacob [and a scepter shall rise out of Israel]*' [Num. 24:17]. From whom will a star come out? From him who is destined to arise from Jacob."

[G] R. Aha in the name of R. Huna, "Esau, the evil one, is destined to put on his cloak and to dwell with the righteous in the Garden of Eden in the age to come. But the Holy One, blessed be he, will drag and throw him out of there."

[H] What is the scriptural basis for this statement?

[I] *"Though you soar aloft like the eagle, though your nest is set among the stars, thence I will bring you down,"* says the Lord [Obad. 4].

[J] And "stars" refers only to the righteous, as you say, *"[And those who are wise shall shine like the brightness of the firmament;] and those who turn many to righteousness, like the stars for ever and ever"* [Dan. 12:3].

The evidence of the Talmud of the Land of Israel thus far has suggested that, in the two centuries beyond the closure of the Mishnah, the generally familiar notion of *the* Messiah who would raise the dead and resolve the problems of Israel's destiny had entered the rabbinic canon. Among authorities who contributed to the Mishnah, this same conventional viewpoint surely circulated, even though the Mishnah itself presents a different and more limited conception of the end.

We come to the crux of matters: what makes a messiah a false messiah? In this Talmud, it is not his claim to save Israel, but his claim to save Israel without the help of God. The meaning of the true Messiah is Israel's total submission, through the Messiah's gentle rule, to God's yoke and service. So God is not to be manipulated through Israel's humoring heaven in rite and cult. The notion of keeping the commandments so as to please heaven and get God to do what Israel wants is totally incongruent to the text at hand. Keeping the commandments as a mark of submission, loyalty, humility before God is the rabbinic system of salvation. So Israel does not "save itself." Israel never controls its own destiny, either on earth or in heaven. The only choice is whether to cast one's fate into the hands of cruel, deceitful men, or to trust in the living God of mercy and love. We shall now see how this critical position is spelled out in the setting of discourse about the Messiah in the Talmud of the Land of Israel.

Bar Kokhba, above all, exemplifies arrogance against God. He lost the war because of that arrogance. In particular, he ignored the authority of sages:

Y. TAANIT 4:5

[X J] Said R. Yohanan, "Upon orders of Caesar Hadrian, they killed eight hundred thousand in Betar."

[K] Said R. Yohanan, "There were eighty thousand pairs of trumpeteers surrounding Betar. Each one was in charge of a number of troops. Ben Kozeba was there and he had two hundred thousand troops who, as a sign of loyalty, had cut off their little fingers.

[L] "Sages sent word to him, 'How long are you going to turn Israel into a maimed people?'

[M] "He said to them, 'How otherwise is it possible to test them?'

[N] "They replied to him, 'Whoever cannot uproot a cedar of Lebanon while riding on his horse will not be inscribed on your military rolls.'

[O] "So there were two hundred thousand who qualified in one way, and another two hundred thousand who qualified in another way."

[P] When he would go forth to battle, he would say, "Lord of the world! Do not help and do not hinder us! *Hast thou not rejected us, O God? Thou dost not go forth, O God, with our armies*'" [Ps. 60:10].

[Q] Three and a half years did Hadrian besiege Betar.

[R] R. Eleazar of Modiin would sit on sackcloth and ashes and pray every day, saying "Lord of the ages! Do not judge in accord with strict judgment this day! Do not judge in accord with strict judgment this day!"

[S] Hadrian wanted to go to him. A Samaritan said to him, "Do not go to him until I see what he is doing, and so hand over the city [of Betar] to you. [Make peace . . . for you.]"

[T] He got into the city through a drain pipe. He went and found R. Eleazar of Modiin standing and praying. He pretended to whisper something into his ear.

[U] The townspeople saw [the Samaritan] do this and brought him to Ben Kozeba. They told him, "We saw this man having dealings with your friend."

[V] [Bar Kokhba] said to him, "What did you say to him, and what did he say to you?"

[W] He said to [the Samaritan], "If I tell you, then the king will kill me, and if I do not tell you, then you will kill me. It is better that the king kill me, and not you.

[X] "[Eleazar] said to me, 'I should hand over my city.' ['I shall make peace . . . .']"

[Y] He turned to R. Eleazar of Modiin. He said to him, "What did this Samaritan say to you?"

[Z] He replied, "Nothing."

[AA] He said to him, "What did you say to him?"

[BB] He said to him, "Nothing."

[CC] [Ben Kozeba] gave [Eleazar] one good kick and killed him.

[DD] Forthwith an echo came forth and proclaimed the following verse:

[EE] "*Woe to my worthless shepherd, who deserts the flock! May the sword smite his arm and his right eye! Let his arm be wholly withered, his right eye utterly blinded!* [Zech. 11:17].

[FF] "You have murdered R. Eleazar of Modiin, the right arm of all Israel, and their right eye. Therefore may the right arm of that man wither, may his right eye be utterly blinded!"

[GG] Forthwith Betar was taken, and Ben Kozeba was killed.

We notice two complementary themes. First, Bar Kokhba treats heaven with arrogance, asking God merely to keep out of the way. Second, he treats an especially revered sage with a parallel arrogance. The sage had the power to preserve Israel. Bar Kokhba destroyed Israel's one protection. The result was inevitable.

Now in noticing the remarkable polemic in the story, in favor of sages' rule over that of Israelite strongmen, we should not lose sight of the importance of the tale for our present argument about the Messiah and history. First, the passage quite simply demonstrates an interest in narrating other events than those involving the Temple or the sages in court. This story and numerous others not quoted here testify to the emergence of a new category of history (or reemergence of an old one), namely, the history not of the supernatural cult but of Israel the people. It indicates that, for the framers of those units of Yerushalmi which are not concerned with Mishnah exegesis, and for the editors who selected materials for the final document, the history of Israel the people had now attained importance and demanded its rightful place. Once Israel's history thus reached center stage, a rich heritage of historical thought would be invoked. Second, the Messiah, the centerpiece of salvation history and hero of the tale, would emerge as a critical figure. The historical theory of this Yerushalmi passage is stated very simply. In their view Israel had to choose between wars, either the war fought by Bar Kokhba or the "war for Torah." "Why had they been punished? It was because of the weight of the war, for they had not wanted to engage in the struggles over the meaning of the Torah" (Y. Ta. 3:9 XVI I). Those struggles, which were ritual arguments about ritual matters, promised the only victory worth winning. Then Israel's history would be written in terms of wars over the meaning of the Torah and the decision of the law.

True, the skins are new, but the wine is very old. For while we speak of sages and learning, the message is the familiar one. It is Israel's history that works out and expresses Israel's relationship with

God. The critical dimension of Israel's life, therefore, is salvation, the definitive trait, a movement in time from now to then. It follows that the paramount and organizing category is history and its lessons. In the Yerushalmi we witness, among the Mishnah's heirs, a striking reversion to biblical convictions about the centrality of history in the definition of Israel's reality. The heavy weight of prophecy, apocalyptic, and biblical historiography, with their emphasis upon salvation and on history as the indicator of Israel's salvation, stood against the Mishnah's quite separate thesis of what truly mattered. What, from their viewpoint, demanded description and analysis and required interpretation? It was the category of sanctification, for eternity. The true issue framed by history and apocalypse was how to move toward the foreordained end of salvation, how to act *in time* to reach salvation *at the end of time*. The Mishnah's teleology beyond time and its capacity to posit an eschatology without a place for a historical Messiah take a position beyond that of the entire antecedent sacred literature of Israel. Only one strand, the priestly one, had ever taken so extreme a position on the centrality of sanctification and the peripheral nature of salvation. Wisdom had stood in between, with its own concerns, drawing attention both to what happened and to what endured. But to Wisdom what finally mattered was not nature or supernature, but rather abiding relationships in historical time.

Disorderly historical events entered the system of the Mishnah and found their place within the larger framework of the Mishnah's orderly world. But to claim that the Mishnah's framers merely ignored what was happening would be incorrect. They worked out their own way of dealing with historical events, the disruptive power of which they not only conceded but freely recognized. Further, the Mishnah's authors did not intend to compose a history book or a work of prophecy or apocalypse. Even if they had wanted to narrate the course of events, they could hardly have done so through the medium of the Mishnah. Yet the Mishnah presents its philosophy in full awareness of the issues of historical calamity confronting the Jewish nation. So far as the philosophy of the document confronts the totality of Israel's existence, the Mishnah by definition *also* presents a philosophy of history.

The Mishnah's subordination of historical events contradicts the emphasis of a thousand years of Israelite thought. The biblical histories, the ancient prophets, the apocalyptic visionaries all had testified that events themselves were important. Events carried the message of the living God. Events constituted history, pointed toward, and so explained, Israel's destiny. An essentially ahistorical system of timeless sanctification, worked out through construction of an eternal rhythm which centered on the movement of the moon and stars and seasons, represented a life chosen by few outside of the priesthood. Furthermore, the pretense that what *happens* matters less than what *is* testified against palpable and memorable reality. Israel had suffered enormous loss of life. As we shall see, the Talmud of the Land of Israel takes these events seriously and treats them as unique and remarkable. The memories proved real. The hopes evoked by the Mishnah's promise of sanctification of a world in static perfection did not. For they had to compete with the grief of an entire century of mourning.

Y. TAANIT 4:5

[X B] Rabbi would derive by exegesis twenty-four tragic events from the verse, "*The Lord has destroyed without mercy all the habitations of Jacob; in his wrath he has broken down the strongholds of the daughter of Judah; he has brought down to the ground in dishonor the kingdom and its rulers*" [Lam. 2:2].
[C] R. Yohanan derived sixty from the same verse.
[D] Did R. Yohanan then find more than Rabbi did in the same verse?
[E] But because Rabbi lived nearer to the destruction of the Temple, there were in the audience old men who remembered what had happened, and when he gave his exegesis, they would weep and fall silent and get up and leave.

We do not know whether things happened as the storyteller says. But the fact remains that the framers of the Yerushalmi preserved the observation that, in Rabbi's time, memory of world-shaking events continued to shape Israel's mind and imagination. For people like those portrayed here, the Mishnah's classification of tragedy cannot have solved many problems.

Accordingly, we should not be surprised to observe that the Talmud of the Land of Israel contains evidence pointing toward substantial steps taken in rabbinical circles away from the position of the Mishnah. We find materials that fall entirely outside the framework of historical doctrine as established within the Mishnah. These are, first, an interest in the periodization of history and, second, a willingness to include events of far greater diversity than those in the Mishnah. So the Yerushalmi contains an expanded view of the range of human life encompassed by the conception of history.

Let us take the second point first. Things happen that demand attention and constitute "events"; within the Mishnah these fall into two classifications, biblical history and events involving the Temple. A glance at the catalogue from M. Ta. 4:6 tells us what kind of happening constitutes an "event," a historical datum demanding attention and interpretation. In this Talmud, by contrast, we find, in addition to Temple events, two other sorts of *Geschichten:* Torah events, that is, important stories about the legal and supernatural doings of rabbis, and also political events.

These events, moreover, involve people not considered in the Mishnah: Gentiles as much as Jews, Rome as much as Israel. The Mishnah's history, such as it is, knows only Israel. The Talmud greatly expands the range of historical interest when it develops a theory of Rome's relationship to Israel, and, of necessity also, Israel's relationship to Rome.

Only by taking account of the world at large can the Talmud's theory of history yield a philosophy of history worthy of the name, that is, an account of who Israel is, the meaning of what happens to Israel, and the destiny of Israel in this world and at the end of time. Israel by itself—as the priests had claimed—lived in eternity, beyond time. Israel and Rome together struggled in historical time—an age with a beginning, a middle, and an end. That is the importance of the expanded range of historical topics found in the present Talmud. When, in the Babylonian Talmud, we find a still broader interest, in Iran as much as Rome and in the sequence of world empires past and present, we see how such a rich and encompassing theory of historical events begins with a simple step toward a universal perspective. It was a step that I think the scribes and priests represented by the Mishnah, unlike the ancient prophets and apocalyptists, were incapable of taking.

The concept of periodization—the raw material of historical thought—hardly presents surprises, since apocalyptic writers began their work by differentiating one age from another. When the Mishnah includes a statement of the "periods" into which time is divided, however, it speaks only of stages of the cult: Shiloh, Nob, Jerusalem. One age is differentiated from the next not by reference to world-historical changes but only by the location of sacrifice and the eating of the victim. The rules governing each locale impose taxa upon otherwise undifferentiated time. So periodization constitutes a function of the larger system of sanctification through sacrifice. The contrast between "this world" and "the world to come," which is not a narrowly historical conception in the Mishnah, now finds a counterpart in the Talmud's contrast between "this age" and the age in which the Temple stood. That distinction is very much an act of this-worldly historical differentiation. It not only yields apocalyptic speculation, but also generates sober and worldly reflection on the movement of events and the meaning of history in the prophetic-apocalyptic tradition. Accordingly, the Talmud of the Land of Israel presents both the expected amplification of the established concepts familiar from the Mishnah and a separate set of ideas, perhaps rooted in prior times but still independent of what the Mishnah in particular had encompassed.

The framers of the Mishnah had found it possible to construct a complete and encompassing teleology for their system with scarcely a single word about the Messiah's coming at that time when the system would be perfectly achieved. So with their interest in explaining events and accounting for history, the third- and fourth-century sages represented in these units of discourse invoked what their predecessors had at best found to be of peripheral consequence to their system. The following contains the most striking expression of this viewpoint.

Y. TAANIT 1:1

[X J] *"The oracle concerning Dumah. One is calling to me from Seir, 'Watchman, what of the night? Watchman, what of the night?'* [Isa. 21:11]."

[K] The Israelites said to Isaiah, "O our Rabbi, Isaiah, what will come for us out of this night?"

[L] He said to them, "Wait for me, until I can present the question."

[M] Once he had asked the question, he came back to them.

[N] They said to him, "Watchman, what of the night? What did the Guardian of the ages tell you?"

[O] He said to them, "The watchman says: *'Morning comes; and also the night. If you will inquire, inquire; come back again'* [Isa. 21:12]."

[P] They said to him, "Also the night?"

[Q] He said to them, "It is not what you are thinking. But there will be morning for the righteous, and night for the wicked, morning for Israel, and night for idolaters."

[R] They said to him, "When?"

[S] He said to them, "Whenever you want, He too wants [it to be]—if you want it, he wants it."

[T] They said to him, "What is standing in the way?"

[U] He said to them, "Repentance: '*Come back again*' [Isa. 21:12]."

[V] R. Aha in the name of R. Tanhum b. R. Hiyya, "If Israel repents for one day, forthwith the son of David will come.

[W] "What is the scriptural basis? '*O that today you would hearken to his voice!*' [Ps. 95:7]."

[X] Said R. Levi, "If Israel would keep a single sabbath in the proper way, forthwith the son of David will come.

[Y] "What is the scriptural basis for this view? '*Moses said, "Eat it today, for today is a sabbath to the Lord; today you will not find it in the field"*' [Exod. 16:25].

[Z] "And it says, '*For thus said the Lord God, the Holy One of Israel, "In returning and rest you shall be saved; in quietness and in trust shall be your strength." And you would not*' [Isa. 30:15]."

A discussion of the power of repentance would hardly have surprised a Mishnah sage. What is new is at V–Z, the explicit linkage of keeping the law with achieving the end of time and the coming of the Messiah. That motif stands separate from the notions of righteousness and repentance, which surely do not require it. So the condition of "all Israel," a social category in historical time, comes under consideration, and not only the status of individual Israelites in life and in death. The latter had formed the arena for the Mishnah's demonstration of its system's meaning. Now history as an operative category, drawing in its wake Israel as a social entity, comes once more on the scene. But, except for the Mishnah's sages, it had never left the stage.

We must not lose sight of the importance of this passage, with its emphasis on repentance, on the one side, and the power of Israel to reform itself, on the other. The Messiah will come any day that Israel makes it possible. If all Israel will keep a single sabbath in the proper (rabbinic) way, the Messiah will come. If all Israel will repent for one day, the Messiah will come. "Whenever you want . . . ," the Messiah will come.

Now, two things are happening here. First, the system of religious observance, including study of Torah, is explicitly invoked as having salvific power. Second, the persistent hope of the people for the coming of the Messiah is linked to the system of rabbinic observance and belief. In this way, the austere program of the Mishnah develops in a different direction, with no trace of a promise that the Messiah will come if and when the system is fully realized. Here a teleology lacking all eschatological dimension gives way to an explicitly messianic statement that the purpose of the law is to attain Israel's salvation: "If you want it, God wants it too." The one thing Israel commands is its own heart; the power it yet exercises is the power to repent. These suffice. The entire history of humanity will respond to Israel's will, to what happens in Israel's heart and soul. With the Temple in ruins, repentance can take place only within the heart and mind.

Let me now summarize this entire discussion of the Messiah and the meaning of history in both the Mishnah and the Talmud of the Land of Israel.

When constructing a systematic account of Judaism—that is, the world view and way of life for Israel presented in the Mishnah—the philosophers of the Mishnah did not make use of the Messiah myth in the construction of a teleology for their system. They found it possible to present a statement of goals for their projected life of Israel which was entirely separate from appeals to history and eschatology. Since they certainly knew, and even alluded to, long-standing and widely held convictions on eschatological subjects, beginning with those in Scripture, the framers thereby testified that, knowing the larger repertoire, they made choices different from others before and after them. Their document accurately and ubiquitously expresses these choices, both affirmative and negative.

The appearance of a messianic eschatology fully consonant with the larger characteristic of the rabbinic system—with its stress on the viewpoints and prooftexts of Scripture, its interest in what was happening to Israel, its focus upon the national-historical dimension of the life of the group—indicates that the encompassing rabbinic system stands essentially autonomous of the prior, mishnaic system. True, what had gone before was absorbed and fully assimilated. But the rabbinic system, expressed in part in each of the non-mishnaic segments of the canon, and fully spelled out in all of them, is different in the aggregate from the mishnaic system. It represents more, however, than a negative response to its predecessor. The rabbinic system took over the fundamental convictions of the Mishnaic world view about the importance of Israel's constructing for itself a life beyond time. The rabbinic system then transformed the Messiah myth in its totality into an essentially ahistorical force. If people wanted to reach the end of time, they had to rise above time, that is, history, and stand off at the side of great movements of political and military character. That is the message of the Messiah myth as it reaches full exposure in the rabbinic system of the two Talmuds. At its foundation it is *precisely* the message of teleology without eschatology expressed by the Mishnah and its associated documents. Accordingly, we cannot claim that the rabbinic system in this regard constitutes a reaction against the mishnaic one. We must conclude, quite to the contrary, that in the Talmuds and their associated documents we see the restatement in classical-mythic form of the ontological convictions that had informed the minds of the second-century philosophers. The new medium contained the old and enduring message: Israel must turn away from time and change, submit to whatever happens, so as to win for itself the only government worth having, that is, God's rule, accomplished through God's anointed agent, the Messiah.

To state matters in unrefined terms, salvation depended upon sanctification, which therefore took precedence as the governing principle of the world view and way of life commanded by the rabbis' Torah. It follows, of course, that the rabbis who stand behind the principles of messianic eschatology, worked out in the Talmuds, in fact continued on an absolutely straight line the fundamental convictions of the Mishnah. That document they claimed to continue and complete. Superficially, that claim is without justification. But at a deeper level it is quite proper.

The Mishnah's framers thus formulated a world view and a way of life for the Jewish nation in which historical events played little part. They insisted on uncovering the continuing patterns of life and the external laws of nature and supernature. To these points, the concept of the Messiah and of the meaning of destiny of Israel among the nations proved irrelevant. The framers of the Mishnah spoke of other things. We do not know to whom they wished to address their vision.

Also, the talmudic continuators of the Mishnah constructed their exegetical essays both *through*, but also *around*, the Mishnah. They explained and expanded upon the Mishnah's points. But they also made provision for expressing their own views, as distinct from those stated in the Mishnah. Do these other, extra-mishnaic, views come later in time? Obviously the answer is partly yes, partly no.

On the one hand, the facts, in the main, can be shown to have circulated before, during, and after the time of the Mishnah's formulation. The first and second centuries, after all, encompassed the greatest messianic explosion in the history of Judaism. Coming at the end, the Mishnah expressed its implacable judgment upon that age of messianic expression. Its authors cannot have failed to know what everyone else in Israel knew full well. So what the Talmud knows about the Messiah, generally, derives from a heritage of facts which had earlier circulated in Israel.

On the other hand, much that the Talmuds' authorities wish to say about these ancient facts and to express through them speaks to a range of conceptions peculiar to the talmudic rabbis themselves. In its particular form and point of insistence, what is distinctive also comes later in the formation of the canon.

So some ideas are general and early and some are particular and late. The governing criterion is special to the canon. What is distinctive to the Mishnah, namely its unfriendly neglect of the Messiah myth, reaches expression early in this canon. What expresses the rabbinical perception of the Messiah reaches its present condition later in the formation of the canon, even though the facts that are reshaped are of ancient origin. So the question is, what in fact happened to the Messiah myth in the canon of rabbinical Judaism in its formative centuries? We turn, now, to this final question.

By reshaping the teleology of the mishnaic system into an eschatological idiom—indeed, by restating the eschatology in the established messianic myth—the rabbis of the Talmud made over the Mishnah's system. But if the Mishnah was thus forced into that very grid of history and eschatology that it had been formulated to reject, the Mishnah's mode of being in turn drastically modified the Messiah myth. For the latter was recast into the philosophical mode of thought and stated as teleology of an eternally present sanctification which was attained by obedience to patterns of holiness laid out in the Torah. This grid is precisely the one that the framers of the Mishnah had defined. By no means may we conclude that what changed, in the end, was the Mishnah's system. Its modes of thought intact, its fundamental points of insistence about Israel's social policy reaffirmed, the Mishnah's system ended up wholly definitive for Judaism as it emerged in the canon at the end of its formative centuries, the "one whole Torah of Moses, our rabbi."

How so? The version of the Messiah myth incorporated into the rabbinic system through the Talmuds simply restates the obvious: Israel's sanctification is what governs. So if Israel will keep a single Sabbath (or two in succession), the Messiah will come. If Israel stops violating the Torah, the Messiah will come. If Israel acts with arrogance in rejecting its divinely assigned condition, the Messiah will not come. Everything depends, then, upon the here-and-now of everyday life. The operative category is not salvation through what Israel *does* but sanctification of what Israel *is*. The fundamental convictions of the Mishnah's framers, flowing from the reaction against the apocalyptic and messianic wars of the late first and early second centuries, here absorbed and redirected precisely those explosive energies that, to begin with, had made Israel's salvation through history the critical concern. So while the Talmuds introduced a formerly neglected myth, their version of the Messiah became precisely what the sages of the Mishnah and their continuators in the Talmud most needed: a rabbi-Messiah, who would save an Israel sanctified through Torah. Salvation then depends upon sanctification, and is subordinated to it.

The Mishnah proposed to build an Israelite world view and way of life that ignored the immediate apocalyptic and historical terrors of the age. The Mishnah's heirs and continuators, who produced the other sector of the formative canon, did two things. They preserved that original policy for Israelite society. But they also accommodated an ongoing social and psychological reality: the presence of terror, the foreboding of doom, and Israel's ironclad faith in the God who saves. Israel remained the old Israel of history, suffering, and hope. The Mishnah's fantasy of an Israel beyond time, an Israel living in nature and supernature, faded away. It was implausible. The facts of history contradicted it.

Yet Israel's condition, moral and social, must govern Israel's destiny —in accordance with the Torah's rules, but also precisely as biblical prophecy and mishnaic doctrine had claimed. What then could Israel do about its own condition? How could Israel confront the unending apocalypse of its own history? Israel could do absolutely nothing. But Israel could be—become—holy. That is why history was relegated to insignificance. Humble acceptance of the harsh rule of Gentiles would render Israel worthy of God's sudden intervention, the institution of God's rule through King-Messiah.

Under the circumstances from that day almost down to our own time, that counsel proved not only good theology but also astute social policy. Until nearly our own time the nations did not oppress Israel "too much," Israel did not rebel "too soon." What the rabbinic canon set forth at the end, in its rich eschatological-messianic myth and symbolism, states precisely what the Mishnah at the outset had defined as its teleology, but in the idiom of life and death, nature and supernature. The rabbinical canon in its ultimate form delivered the message of sanctification, garbed in the language of salvation—but not garbled by that expression.

To end where we began, Judaism in its formative canon does not fall into the classification of a messianic religion. It makes use of messianic materials to make its own statement. That statement, never intact but always unimpaired, speaks for the Mishnah. If the hands are the hands of the inherited eschatological faith of prophecy and apocalypse, the voice remains the true voice of Jacob.

PART THREE: METHOD

TORAH, CANON, SAGE

9

Revelation and Canon

When revelation stops, what then? The issue confronts Judaism and Christianity, in particular, because both religious communities receive and live by the statement of God's will to Moses and the prophets. Standing in direct succession to Sinai, Judaism speaks about a holy life framed in accord with God's will revealed in the Torah. Affirming and claiming to appropriate the entire heritage of ancient Israel and Judaism to its time, Christianity in nearly all its forms speaks of fulfilling the law and the prophets in the person of Jesus and the salvation of Christ. Accordingly, for Judaism and Christianity, the statement of God to Moses and the prophets stands for a single word, but with a double meaning: both then and now. That is to say, both religious traditions speak about God's will now, not merely revelation then. Both affirm an ongoing relationship between God and Israel—after the flesh, after the spirit—in which revelation of God's will and word endures as a fact of life.

But then revelation does *not* stop. For Judaism God's will is ever present. God now speaks, in the Torah today, as always in the past. For Christianity in its diverse traditions God endures in the Church, in tradition, in the preaching of the Word. And therein, for both faiths, we uncover the enduring dilemma. If God speaks through Torah, then, for Judaism, the issue turns upon what we receive or define as Torah. What finds room in the canon? And just how and to whom does God speak? The issue of ongoing encounter with the living God and of life in accord with the word of God joins to the definition of the canon of Torah. That is, what do we admit and what exclude?

For Judaism and Christianity the presence of the Hebrew Scriptures, which Jews know as Tanakh (for the biblical writings of the Pentateuch, Torah, hence T; prophets, Nebiim, hence N; and writings, Ketubim, hence K), and Christians as the Old Testament, presents no answer to the question of canon. Rather Israel's Scriptures press the deeper question and frame the dilemma. For once people recognize that there is a Tanakh or an Old Testament, that is, a finished scripture, the issue of the place and relationship of all subsequent revelation, both written and not written, comes to acute formulation. If *torah*, in the sense of revelation, becomes *The Torah*, a particular set of compositions, then one must wonder whether revelation has come to an end. Can there be more Torahs, more Sinais? If there is a completed Testament, then the place and role we might define for a further testament demand attention. So the existence of a completed document of revelation presents, in chronic form, the dilemma about the authority and standing of further revelations later on.

The dilemma reaches an acute stage when new holy books, records of revelation, take shape and demand admission to the canon. The demand turns out to be irresistible when the consensus of believers bestows upon the new books the status of revelation, the standing of sanctification. Now it is one thing to interpret and apply the existing revelation to a new situation. Exegesis and amplification present no break with existing Scripture but confirm it. It is quite another to reckon with writings outside of the established canon, yet widely understood to contain not merely more words of faith and truth, but God's word too. Accordingly, the life of faith, assuredly rich in encounter with the living God, has perpetually to present new fruits for that compendious basket we know as the canon: the authoritative documents of the faith. So far as Judaism and Christianity abide, the issue of the interplay between old and new, canon and ongoing writing down of revelation, lives and vivifies. That is the issue before us.

The advent of the Mishnah in ca. 200 C.E. demanded that people explain the status and authority of the new document. In consequence, in the Judaism of rabbis the canon of the religion of Israel had reopened. It would remain eternally open, for *torah* would encom-

pass rabbis' teachings for all time to come. Accordingly, the conception of the form and possibilities of revelation reached wholly fresh
definition. As we shall see, moreover, the lines of structure emanating
from the Mishnah led to the formation of a vast and unprecedented
literature of Judaism. The explosive force of the return to Zion, in the
time of Ezra, had produced the formation of the Torah-book and
much else. The extraordinary impact of the person and message of
Jesus (among other things) had led to the creation of an unprecedented kind of writing in a sector of Israel's life. So too would be the
case with the Mishnah.

The Mishnah is a vast set of statements about what Israel, the
Jewish people, is supposed to do on its farms and in its homes, in the
Temple in Jerusalem and in the courts of its villages, on ordinary days
and on the Sabbath and festival days. It is a kind of law code, in that it
contains statements that say what one does. It is a kind of schoolbook,
in that it presents many opinions about what in theory we are supposed to do. If you study the deeper issues underlying many statements in the Mishnah, furthermore, you find that the sages confront
perennial issues of philosophy, expressed in concrete and humble
details. It is as if they prefer to talk about the acorn and the oak than
potentiality and actuality. So the Mishnah in all is a philosophical
essay, rich in theoretical initiatives, which also serves as a law code.

The reason the document proved decisive in the history of Judaism,
from its time to ours, is that, to begin with, it enjoyed the sponsorship
of the autonomous ruler of the Jewish nation in the Land of Israel,
namely, Judah, the Patriarch, with the result that the Mishnah served
for purposes other than simply learning and speculative thought. At
its very beginnings the Mishnah was turned into an authoritative law
code, the constitution, along with Scripture, of Israel in its Land.
Accordingly, when completed, the Mishnah emerged from the
schoolhouse and forthwith made its move into the politics, courts, and
bureaus of the Jewish government of the Land of Israel. Men who
mastered the Mishnah thereby qualified themselves as judges and
administrators in the government of Judah the patriarch, as well as in
the government of the Jewish community of Babylonia. Over the next
three hundred years, the Mishnah served as the foundation for the
formation of the system of law and theology we now know as Judaism.

The vast collection constituted by the Mishnah therefore de-

manded explanation: What is this book? How does it relate to the
(written) Torah revealed to Moses at Mount Sinai? Under whose
auspices, and by what authority, does the law of the Mishnah govern
the life of Israel? These questions, we realize, bear both political and
theological implications. But, to begin with, the answers emerge out
of an enterprise of exegesis, of literature. The reception of the Mishnah followed several distinct lines, each of them symbolized by a
particular sort of book. Each book, in turn, offered its theory of the
origin, character, and authority of the Mishnah. For the next three
centuries these theories would occupy the attention of the best minds
of Israel, the authorities of the two Talmuds and the numerous other
works of the age of the seed-time of Judaism.

One line from the Mishnah stretched through the Tosefta, a supplement to the Mishnah, and the two Talmuds, one formed in the Land
of Israel, the other in Babylonia, both serving as exegesis and amplification of the Mishnah.

The second line stretched from the Mishnah to compilations of
biblical exegesis of three different sorts. First, there were exegetical
collections framed in relationship to the Mishnah, in particular Sifra,
on Leviticus, Sifré on Numbers, and Sifré on Deuteronomy. Second,
exegetical collections were organized in relationship to Scripture,
with special reference to Genesis and Leviticus. Third, exegetical
collections focused on constructing abstract discourse out of diverse
verses of Scripture but on a single theme or problem, represented by
Pesikta de Rab Kahana.

This simple catalogue of the types, range, and volume of creative
writing over the three hundred years from the closure of the Mishnah
indicates an obvious fact. The Mishnah stands at the beginning of a
new and stunningly original epoch in the formation of Judaism. Like
the return to Zion and the advent of Jesus in Israel, the Mishnah
ignited a great burst of energy. The extraordinary power of the
Mishnah, moreover, is seen in its very lonely position in Israelite holy
literature. The entire subsequent literature refers back to the Mishnah
or stands in some clearcut hermeneutical relationship to it. But for its
part, the Mishnah refers to nothing prior to itself—except (and then,
mostly implicitly and by indirection) to Scripture. So from the Mishnah back to the revelation of God to Moses at Sinai—in the view of
the Mishnah—lies a vast desert. But from the Mishnah forward
stretches a fertile plain.

The crisis precipitated by the Mishnah therefore stimulated wide-ranging speculation, inventive experiments of a literary and (in the nature of things) therefore also political, theological, and religious character. The Talmuds' work of defining and explaining the Mishnah in relationship to the (written) Torah, interpreting the meaning of the Mishnah, expanding upon and applying its laws, ultimately yielded the making, also, of compilations of the exegeses of Scripture. The formation of the Talmuds and exegetical collections thus made necessary—indeed, urgent—extraordinary and original reflection on the definition of canon, the nature of scriptural authority, and the range and possibilities of revelation. The results of that work all together would then define Judaism from that time to this. So the crisis presented an opportunity. And Israel's sages took full advantage of the occasion. That, in a word, is the story before us. What then was this crisis?

Let me begin the tale by returning to the Mishnah itself. I have first of all to explain why and how the Mishnah presented such an unprecedented problem to the patriarch's sages who received the Mishnah. It is easy to do so in a way accessible to people to whom all of these events and writings have been, up to now, entirely unknown or, if known, alien and incomprehensible. To phrase the theological question so that anyone in the West may grasp it, I need simply point out one fact. So far as Judaism was concerned, revelation had been contained in the Tanakh, the written Torah. True, God may have spoken in diverse ways. But revelation had come down in only one form, in writing. The last of the biblical books had been completed—so far as Jews then knew—many centuries before. How then could a new book now claim standing as holy and revealed by God? What validated the authority of the people who knew and applied that holy book to Israel's life? These questions, as we shall see, would define the critical issue of formative Judaism, from 200 to 600 C.E. The resolution of the problem defines Judaism today. Accordingly, the crisis precipitated by the Mishnah came about because of the urgent requirement of explaining, first, just what the Mishnah was in relationship to the Torah of Moses; second, why the sages who claimed to interpret and apply the law of the Mishnah to the life of Israel had the authority to do so; and, third, how Israel, in adhering to the rules of the Mishnah, kept the will of God and lived the holy life God wanted them to live.

But why should the Mishnah in particular have presented these critical problems of a social and theological order? After all, it was hardly the first piece of new writing to confront Israel from the closure of Scripture to the end of the second century. Other books had found a capacious place in the canon of the groups of Israelites that received them and deemed them holy. The canon of some groups, after all, had made room for those writings of apocryphal and pseud-epigraphic provenance so framed as to be deemed holy. The Essene library at Qumran encompassed a diverse group of writings, surely received as authoritative and holy, that other Jews did not know within their canon. So we have to stand back and ask why, to the sages who received and realized the Mishnah, that book should have pre-sented special, particularly stimulating, problems. Why should the issue of the relationship of the Mishnah to Scripture have proved so pressing in the third, fourth, and fifth centuries' circles of talmudic rabbis? After all, we have no evidence that the relationship to the canon of Scripture of the Manual of Discipline, the Hymns, the War Scroll, or the Damascus Covenant perplexed the teacher of right-eousness and the other holy priests of the Essene community. To the contrary, those documents at Qumran appear side by side with the ones we now know as canonical Scripture. The high probability is that, to the Essenes, the sectarian books were no less holy and author-itative than Leviticus, Deuteronomy, Nahum, Habakkuk, Isaiah, and the other books of the biblical canon they, among all Israelites, revered.

The issue, as we shall shortly see, had to be raised because of the peculiar traits of the Mishnah itself. But the dilemma proved acute, not merely chronic, because of the particular purpose the Mishnah was meant to serve, and because of the political sponsorship behind the document. As I said above, it was to provide Israel's constitution. It was promulgated by the patriarch—the ethnic ruler—of the Jewish nation in the Land of Israel, Judah the Patriarch, who ruled with Roman support as the fully recognized Jewish authority in the Holy Land. So the Mishnah was public, not sectarian, nor merely idle speculation of a handful of Galilean rabbinical philosophers, though, in structure and content, that is precisely what it was. It was a political document. It demanded assent and conformity to its rules, where they were relevant to the government and court system of the Jewish people in its land. So the Mishnah could not be ignored and therefore had to be explained in universally accessible terms. Furthermore, the

Mishnah demanded explanation not merely in relationship to the established canon of Scripture and apology as the constitution of the Jew's government, the patriarchate of second-century Land of Israel. The nature of Israelite life, lacking all capacity to distinguish as secular any detail of the common culture, made it natural to wonder about a deeper issue. Israel understood its collective life and the fate of each individual under the aspect of God's loving concern, as expressed in the Torah. Accordingly, laws issued to define what people were supposed to do could not stand by themselves; they had to receive the imprimatur of Heaven, that is, they had to be given the status of revelation. Accordingly, to make its way in Israelite life, the Mishnah as a constitution and code demanded for itself a theory of beginnings at (or relationship to) Sinai, with Moses, from God. As was pointed out above, other new writings for a long time had proved able to win credence as part of the Torah, hence as revealed by God and so enjoying legitimacy. But they did so in ways not taken by the Mishnah's framers. How did the Mishnah differ?

It was in the medium of writing that, in the view of all of Israel until about 200 C.E., God had been understood to reveal the divine word and will. The Torah was a written book. People who claimed to receive further messages from God usually wrote them down. They had three choices in securing acceptance of their account. All three involved linking the new to the old. In claiming to hand on revelation, they could, first, sign their books with the names of biblical heroes. Second, they could imitate the style of biblical Hebrew. Third, they could present an exegesis of existing written verses, validating their ideas by supplying proof-texts for them.

From the closure of the Torah literature in the time of Ezra, ca. 450 B.C.E., to the time of the Mishnah, nearly seven hundred years later, we do not have a single book alleged to be holy and at the same time standing wholly out of relationship to the Holy Scriptures of ancient Israel. The pseudepigraphic writings fall into the first category, the Essene writings at Qumran into the second and third. We may point to the Gospels, which take as a principal problem demonstrating how Jesus had fulfilled the prophetic promises of the Old Testament and in other ways carried forward and even embodied Israel's Scripture.

Insofar as a piece of Jewish writing did not find a place in relationship to Scripture, its author laid no claim to present a holy book. The contrast between Jubilees and the Testaments of the Patriarchs, with their constant and close harping on biblical matters, and the several books of Maccabees, shows the difference. The former claim to present revealed truth, the latter, history. So a book was holy because in style, in authorship, or in (alleged) origin, it continued Scripture, finding a place therefore (at least in the author's mind) within the canon, or because it provided an exposition of Scripture's meaning.

But the Mishnah made no such claim. It entirely ignored the style of biblical Hebrew, speaking in a quite different kind of Hebrew altogether. It is silent on its authorship through sixty-two of the sixty-three tractates (the claims of Abot pose a special problem). In any event, nowhere does the Mishnah contain the claim that God had inspired the authors of the document. These are not given biblical names and certainly are not alleged to have been biblical saints. Most of the book's named authorities flourished within the same century as its anonymous arrangers and redactors, not in remote antiquity. Above all, the Mishnah contains scarcely a handful of exegeses of Scripture. These, where they occur, play a trivial and tangential role. So here is the problem of the Mishnah: different from Scripture in language and style, indifferent to the claim of authorship by a biblical hero or divine inspiration, stunningly aloof from allusion to verses of Scripture for nearly the whole of its discourse—yet authoritative for Israel. How come?

Still more vividly to grasp the dilemma presented by the Mishnah, we move far from the time and place of ancient Israel in 200 C.E. We take up the problem of revelation as received by a culture in the South Seas in nearly our own time.

Just how does God speak to us? When a shift takes place in the medium of revelation, it is a symptom that a far more profound turning in the formation of culture has been reached. Sam D. Gill, in *Beyond "the Primitive": The Religions of Non-Literate Peoples* (Englewood Cliffs, N.J.: Prentice-Hall, 1982) 102, points out that, in the precolonial way of life, peoples of Oceania and Melanesia referred to stories of origins to reveal the patterns of their culture, and relied "upon the spiritual communication with ancestors and deities to maintain a fertile and creative life in the physical world. Spiritual communication was essential to life." This took place through dreams and visions. Then, Gill says, the advent of the Europeans, with a quite different form of communication, changed everything. He notes,

"Missionaries dwelt heavily upon the written word as the means of the revelation of God, and the colonial administration used writing to maintain contact with its home country, the source of its supplies. . . . [Literacy] was accepted as a spiritual mode of communication." Accordingly, the move from one medium of heavenly communication to another both precipitated a crisis and served as one of the symptoms of that crisis.

That fact is important to us, for, as we shall see in a little while, one of the principal theories of the origins of the Mishnah and vindications of its authority lay in the allegation that it constituted revelation, but in a different mode of communication from writing. Namely, it was revelation preserved in oral formulation and oral transmission, through memorization and repetition. For the moment, it suffices to prepare the way to a full appreciation of the problem posed by the Mishnah by noting that, until then, whatever other groups of Israelites laid claim to revelation took for granted that, like the revelation contained in the Hebrew Scriptures, a fair part of any further revelation would be written down.

Thus far we have noted that, in time to come, the Mishnah would find one principal justification and apology in the claim that it constituted oral tradition, going back to Moses at Sinai. To that remarkable claim we have now to join yet a second unusual trait of the Mishnah. The Mishnah is something like a law code. Accordingly, when we turn to the law codes of ancient Israel, we notice traits we have every reason to find, also, in the Mishnah. The first and most important of these is the telling of a tale to explain the authority and standing of the code and its laws. The Covenant Code (Ex. 20:22—23:33), for instance, starts with God's telling Moses to tell Israel, "You have seen for yourselves that I have talked with you from heaven." So all the laws that follow come from God in heaven. The Priestly Code iterates and reiterates the formula, "The Lord called Moses and spoke to him. . . ." The vast law collection in Deuteronomy begins only after a great address on the giving of the law has explained the origin and sanction of the law. Accordingly, Israel had every reason to expect that a law code would carry along its own myth of origin and authority. Later lawyers were quick to supply such myths. The framers of the so-called Damascus Rule of the Essene Community at Qumran begin with a long exhortation, introducing the authority of the code, the teacher of righteousness, retelling the sacred history of Israel, and only then presenting the detailed laws. The Community Rule or Manual of Discipline starts with the statement that if people live in accord with the Book of the Community Rule, then they "may seek God with a whole heart and soul and do what is good and right before Him as He commanded by the hand of Moses and all his servants the prophets, that they may love all he has chosen and hate all that he has rejected" (G. Vermes, *The Dead Sea Scrolls in English* [Gloucester, Mass.: Peter Smith, 1975], 72). When, in a different setting altogether, people proposed to tell the story of Jesus, the Christ, they began by explaining who they were and how they knew what they knew, or who Jesus was and where he came from, or both. So, in a word, it was normal in Israelite culture to write books and to expect God to write books or dictate them. It was routine to provide an account of the origin of a book, to supply a myth of heavenly authority for a law code in particular. The Mishnah does not bother.

Precisely how the Mishnah inaugurates an unprecedented age in the literature of Judaism should be obvious to the reader from these points of emphasis in the preceding paragraphs. Let us now review where we stand in the unfolding argument of this book.

First, once closed and promulgated, the Mishnah would gain from its earliest apologists a myth of oral formulation and oral transmission through processes of memorization, a claim unusual in Israel, to which, for millennia, God had been conceived as communicating in writing.

Second, the Mishnah itself contains no myth of its origin in heaven, no account of its purpose, no claim or promise of the redemption of Israel through keeping its laws. (Abot 1:1–18 hardly presents a counterpart to Deut. 1:1ff.!)

Third, it already is clear that, in style, the Mishnah simply bypasses all of the aesthetic conventions of religious conviction commonplace among earlier Israelite writers, not bearing the name of a known, ancient authority, not imitating the style of biblical law codes or even their language, and not even providing its laws with an exegetical basis in relationship to biblical texts.

Fourth, had the Mishnah emerged from a circle of sectarians off in some wilderness plain, the Jewish nation at large need not have paid much attention to it. But the Mishnah comes down to us not through the medium of archaeology but through the living world of Judaism. So it clearly overcame the limits of sectarianism. Indeed, from the moment of closure and promulgation, the Mishnah enjoyed remarkable status. The Mishnah constituted the authoritative law code of Israel, the Jewish nation, living in its own land, the Land of Israel, and governed by its own authorities, the sages, or rabbis, of Israel, through the sponsorship of its own, internationally recognized ruler, the patriarch (*nasi*) of Israel. That, at least, is what the exegeses attached to the Mishnah, called the Talmuds, tell us. It is what every book of history about the world of Jewry and Judaism, from 200 C.E. onward, records.

So the Mishnah was not a statement of theory alone, telling us only how things will be in the eschaton. Nor was it a wholly sectarian document, reporting the view of a group without standing or influence in the larger life of Israel. True, in some measure it bears both of these traits. But the Mishnah was and is law for Israel. It entered the government and courts of the Jewish people, both in the motherland and also overseas, as the authoritative constitution of the courts of Judaism. The advent of the Mishnah therefore marked a turning in the life of the nation-religion. The document demanded explanation and apology.

The one thing you could not do, as a Jew in third-century Tiberias, Sepphoris, Caesarea, or Beth Shearim, in Galilee, was ignore the thing. True, you might refer solely to ancient Scripture and tradition and live out your life within the inherited patterns of the familiar Israelite religion-culture. But as soon as you dealt with the Jewish government in charge of your everyday life—went to court over the damages done to your crop by your neighbor's ox, for instance—you came up against a law in addition to the law of Scripture, a document the principles of which governed and settled all matters. So the Mishnah rapidly came to confront the life of Israel. The people who knew the Mishnah, the rabbis or sages, came to dominate that life. And their claim, in accord with the Mishnah, to exercise authority and the right to impose heavenly sanction came to perplex. Now the crisis should be fully exposed.

The sages in charge of Israel's courts and bureaucracy would spend three hundred years resolving that crisis, figuring out how to receive this new thing, this Mishnah. Receiving the Mishnah meant setting it into relationship with the ancient Scriptures. Let me now, in a single sentence, report what they did. The sages totally reformed the meaning of the word *Torah*, thereby, in the literary framework, reopening

the canon of Judaism, and, in the theological setting, redefining the
meaning and limits of revelation. The literary result would be the
whole of talmudic literature, on the one side, and, later on, the
formation of the earliest compilations of exegeses (the *midrashim*).
The theological result would be Judaism as we know it: a living and
enduring faith of everyday encounter with God through Torah and
its holy way of life. Rabbis thus reshaped the meaning of the word
Torah by exegetical processes which, to begin with, linked the statements of the Mishnah to verses of Scripture. The exegetical work, in
consequence, overspread its original boundaries—the Mishnah—and
encompassed Scripture within modes of exegesis and discourse of
exactly the same taxonomic character.

So the Mishnah made necessary the formation of the Talmuds, its
exegetical companions. Within the processes of exegesis of the Mishnah came the labor of collecting and arranging these exegeses, in
correlation with the Mishnah, read line by line and paragraph by
paragraph. The sorts of things the sages who framed the Talmud did
to the Mishnah, they then went and did to Scripture. Within the work
of exegesis of Scripture was the correlative labor of organizing what
had been said verse by verse, following the structure of a book of the
Hebrew Bible. The type of discourse and the mode of organizing the
literary result of discourse which were suitable for the one document
served the other too. The same people did both for the same reasons.

10

Scripture and the Mishnah

Formally, redactionally, and linguistically the Mishnah stands in splendid isolation from Scripture. It is not possible to point in prior Israelite religious writing to many parallels, that is, cases of anonymous books, received as holy, in which the forms and formulations (specific verses) of Scripture play so slight a role. People who wrote holy books commonly imitated the Scripture's language. They cited concrete verses. They claimed at the very least that direct revelation had come to them, as in the angelic discourses of IV Ezra and Baruch, so that what they say stands on an equal plane with Scripture. The internal evidence of the Mishnah's sixty-two usable tractates (excluding Abot), by contrast, in no way suggests that anyone pretended to talk like Moses and write like Moses, claimed to cite and correctly interpret things that Moses had said, or even alleged to have had a revelation like that of Moses and so to stand on the mountain with Moses. There is none of this. So the claim of scriptural authority for the Mishnah's doctrines and institutions is difficult to locate within the internal evidence of the Mishnah itself.

Let us now rapidly survey the conceptual relationships between various Mishnah tractates, on the one side, and laws of Scripture, on the other.

First, there are tractates which simply repeat in their own words precisely what Scripture has to say, and at best serve to amplify and complete the basic ideas of Scripture. For example, all of the cultic tractates of the second division, on Appointed Times, which tell what one is supposed to do in the Temple on the various special days of the year, and the bulk of the cultic tractates of the fifth division, which deals with Holy Things, simply restate facts of Scripture. For another example, all of those tractates of the sixth division, on Purities, which specify sources of uncleanness, completely depend on information supplied by Scripture. Every important statement, for example, in Niddah, on menstrual uncleanness, the most fundamental notions of Zabim, on the uncleanness of the person with flux referred to in Leviticus 15, as well as every detail in Negaim, on the uncleanness of the person or house suffering the uncleanness described at Leviticus 13 and 14—all of these tractates serve only to reiterate the basic facts of Scripture and to complement those facts with other derivative ones.

There are, second, tractates which take up facts of Scripture but work them out in a way that those scriptural facts could not have led us to predict. A supposition concerning what is important about the facts, utterly remote from the supposition of Scripture, will explain why the Mishnah tractates under discussion say the original things they say in confronting those scripturally-provided facts. For one example, Scripture (Num. 19:1ff.) takes for granted that the red cow will be burned in a state of uncleanness, because it is burned outside the camp (Temple). The priestly writers cannot have imagined that a state of cultic cleanness was to be attained outside of the cult. The absolute datum of Mishnah-tractate Parah, on burning the red cow, by contrast, is that cultic cleanness not only can be attained outside of the "tent of meeting"; the red cow was to be burned in a state of cleanness even exceeding the cultic cleanness required in the Temple itself. The problematic which generates the intellectual agendum of Parah, therefore, is how to work out the conduct of the rite of burning the cow in relationship to the Temple: Is it to be done in exactly the same way, or in exactly the opposite way? This mode of contrastive and analogical thinking helps us to understand the generative problematic of such tractates as Erubin and Besah, to mention only two.

Third, there are, predictably, many tractates which either take up problems in no way suggested by Scripture, or begin from facts at best merely relevant to facts of Scripture. In the former category are Tohorot, on the cleanness of foods, with its companion, Uqsin; Demai, on doubtfully tithed produce; Tamid, on the conduct of the daily whole-offering; Baba Batra, on rules of real estate transactions and certain other commercial and property relationships, and so on. Representative of the latter category is Ohalot, which spins out its strange problems within the theory that a tent and a utensil are to be compared to one another (!). Other instances are these: Kelim, on the susceptibility to uncleanness of various sorts of utensils; Miqvaot, on the sorts of water which effect purification from uncleanness; Ketubot and Gittin, on the documents of marriage and divorce; and many others. These tractates here and there draw facts of Scripture. But the problem confronted in these tractates—the generative problematic—in no way responds to issues or even facts important to Scripture. What we have here is a prior program of inquiry, which will make ample provision for facts of Scripture in an inquiry generated, to begin with, essentially outside of the framework of Scripture. First comes the problem or topic, then, if possible, attention to Scripture.

So there we have it: some tractates merely repeat what we find in Scripture. Some are totally independent of Scripture. And some fall in-between. We find everything and its opposite. But to offer a final answer to the question of Scripture-Mishnah relationships, we have to take that fact seriously. The Mishnah in no way is so remote from Scripture as its formal omission of citations of verses of Scripture suggests. It also cannot be described as contingent upon, and secondary to Scripture, as many of its third-century apologists claimed. But the right answer is not that it is somewhere in-between. Scripture confronts the framers of the Mishnah as revelation, not merely as a source of facts. But the framers of the Mishnah had their own world with which to deal. They made statements in the framework and fellowship of their own age and generation. They were bound, therefore, to come to Scripture with a set of questions generated elsewhere than in Scripture. They brought their own ideas about what was going to be important in Scripture. This is perfectly natural.

The philosophers of the Mishnah conceded to Scripture the highest authority. At the same time what they chose to hear, within the authoritative statements of Scripture, would in the end form a statement of its own. To state matters simply: all of Scripture was authoritative. But only some of Scripture was found to be relevant. And what happened is that the framers and philosophers of the tradition of the Mishnah came to Scripture when they had reason to. That is to say, they brought to Scripture a program of questions and inquiries framed essentially among themselves. So they were highly selective.

That is why their program itself constituted a statement *upon* the meaning of Scripture. They and their apologists of one sort hastened to add that their program consisted of a statement *of*, and not only upon, the meaning of Scripture.

The way in which the sages of the Mishnah utilized the inherited and authoritative tradition of Scripture therefore is clear. On the one hand, wherever they could, they repeated what Scripture says. This they did, however, in their own words. So they established a claim of relevance and also authority. They spoke to their own day in their own idiom. On the other hand, they selected with care and precision what they wanted in Scripture, ignoring what they did not want. They took up laws, not prophecies, descriptions of how things are supposed to be, not accounts of what is going to happen.

So much for the role of Scripture in the Mishnah. We turn now to ask how the heirs and continuators of the Mishnah, the rabbinical sages who inherited the document after ca. 200 C.E., sorted out the diverse questions before them, the questions of (1) canon, (2) scriptural authority, and (3) revelation. Specifically, they had to make a judgment on the place and authority of the Mishnah within the total corpus of revelation called, in Judaism, "the Torah." Second, in order to reach such an assessment, they further had to impose their own view, through exegesis of the Mishnah, about the place and authority of Scripture within the Mishnah, forming a concomitant position on the relationship of the Mishnah to Scripture. Let us now review the principal documents produced in the rabbinical estate after the closure of the Mishnah.

Three different kinds of literature flow from the Mishnah and refer to it. One, Tosefta, supplements to the Mishnah, is a wholly dependent, secondary, and exegetical form, in which the Mishnah provides the whole frame of organization and redaction for all materials, and in which citation and secondary expansion of the statements of the Mishnah define the bulk, though not the whole, of the work. The next, Sifra, exegeses of Leviticus, focuses not upon the Mishnah but upon Scripture and proposes to provide a bridge between the two. Sifra, and to a lesser degree, Sifré to Numbers and Sifré to Deuteronomy, fall into this second category. The last is in the middle, both dependent upon and autonomous of the Mishnah, taking up its individual statements and amplifying them, but also expanding and developing autonomous discussions. The two Talmuds, one produced in the Land of Israel, the other in Babylonia, constitute this kind of writing. We need briefly to consider how each of these kinds of literature defines the role of Scripture in the Mishnah.

How to pave the road from the Mishnah to Scripture? The answer lay in one age-old and commonplace mode of dealing with precisely the same problem. A conventional way of reading Scripture commonly called *midrash* and here called simply *exegesis*, had long proved acceptable. Why change now? Israelite thinkers—whether lawyers and philosophers, like the heirs of the Mishnah in the Talmuds, or visionaries and prophets, like the Essenes at Qumran, or messianists and evangelists, like the members of the school of Matthew—routinely read one thing in relationship to something else, old Scripture in the setting of fresh concerns and sure knowledge of new truth. So there is nothing remarkable in what the heirs of the Mishnah did. To seek, through biblical exegesis, to link the Mishnah to Scripture, detail by detail, represented a well-trodden and firmly-packed path.

What captures our attention is not the techniques of exegesis but, in particular, the place and purpose assigned to the larger labor of exegesis. To the Tosefta, Sifra, and Talmud of the Land of Israel alike, the paramount issue was Scripture, not merely its authority, but especially, its sheer mass of information. The decisive importance of the advent of the Mishnah in precipitating the vast exegetical enterprise represented by the books at hand emerges from a simple fact. The three documents before us all focus attention on the Mishnah in particular. Two of them, the Tosefta and the Talmud of the Land of Israel (not to mention the other, larger Talmud, made in Babylonia) organize everything at hand around the redactional structure supplied by the Mishnah itself. The third's—Sifra's—obsession with the Mishnah is still more blatant.

For it is all the more striking what the redactional choice of the Sifra's framers called to the fore: the selection of a book of Scripture, rather than of the Mishnah, as the focus for exegesis. That choice conforms entirely to the polemic of the writers and compilers of the Sifra: Scripture is important, the Mishnah subordinate. How better say so than organize things not around the Mishnah, but around a book of the law of Moses itself? So the Mishnah now is cited in a work about Scripture. Let me unpack this point. Down to the editing of the Sifra, Scripture had been cited in works on the Mishnah. Since the

Sifra draws upon materials of the Mishnah and the Tosefta, we have every reason to suppose the redactors of the Sifra knew full well the ways taken by others. They rejected those ways, reversing the redactional convention based on the Mishnah's structure and choosing what was, in context, a fresh and different route. To be sure, that way, in the setting of antecedent Judaism, had been entirely familiar. Earlier writers had laid out their exegesis of Scripture side by side with a text of Scripture. So doing things the way the Sifra's composers did the work was nothing new. Earlier writers also had expressed their own ideas through their arrangement of verses of Scripture.

But the Mishnah is the first document of its kind of Judaism. Afterwards, the Tosefta and the Talmud came along—probably at roughly the same time. Their materials derived both from the period in which the Mishnah was taking shape and also from the period after which the Mishnah had reached closure. And, it would seem, the Sifra comes later on, surely after both the Mishnah and the Tosefta. Its assertions are more extreme, its redactional definition more radical. There is a correspondence, therefore, between the kind of material that is collected and the way that material is arranged. The polemical purposes of the document are expressed not only in what is said, but in how what is said is collected and arranged. Since I wish to place into the context established by the formation of the Talmud of the Land of Israel the labor of collecting and arranging the earliest compilations of scriptural exegesis—the compositions of the fifth and sixth centuries—I have now to stand back. My thesis, as is clear, now may be expressed as a simple formula:

$$\frac{\text{Talmud}}{\text{Mishnah}} = \frac{\text{Exegetical Collection}}{\text{Scripture}}$$

To put the matter in words, Genesis Rabbah on Genesis is to be compared to a Talmud tractate devoted to a particular tractate of the Mishnah.

11

Revelation, Canon, and Scriptural Authority: (1) The Historical and the Apologetic Context

The path from literary analysis to religious insight leads through the history of the community. The context addressed by the sacred writings, old and new, and sustained by the theological convictions and religious experience contained in them, defines the issues, so governs the content of the faith. To speak of the Torah of Israel, therefore, we have first to address the condition of the nation of Israel, the Jewish people. Accordingly, to interpret conviction, we begin with a description of context. True, conviction resists reduction to the status of a mere function of circumstance. Truth is truth. Revelation is not contained in what merely takes place by accident in time. But the believing community wrote books in some one place, at some specific time, not elsewhere and on another day. So we have to ask ourselves, why at just this time and in just this place did sages (or some of them) think it important to say just what they said to Israel? And first we have to speak of who the people of Israel were, and what was happening to them, in that place and in that day, in which rabbis made the statements now before us.

For nearly everyone in the Roman world the most important events of the fourth and fifth centuries, the period in which the Talmud of the Land of Israel and collections of exegeses were coming into being, were, first, the legalization of Christianity, followed very rapidly by the adoption of Christianity as the state's most favored religion, and then by the delegitimization of paganism (and systematic degradation of Judaism). The astonishing advent of legitimacy and even power provoked Christian intellectuals to rewrite Christian and world history and work out theology in reflection on this new polity and its meaning in the unfolding of human history. A new commonwealth was coming into being, taking over the old and reshaping it for the new age. In 312 C.E. Constantine achieved power in the West. In 323 he took the government of the entire Roman Empire into his own hands. He had promulgated the edict of Milan in 313, whereby Christianity attained the status of toleration. Christians and all others were given "the free power to follow the religion of their choice." In the next decade Christianity became the most favored religion. Converts from Judaism were protected and could not be punished by Jews. Christians were freed of the obligation to perform pagan sacrifices. Priests were exempted from certain taxes. Sunday became an obligatory day of rest. Celibacy was permitted. From 324 onward Constantine ceased to maintain a formal impartiality, now intervening in the affairs of the Church, settling quarrels among believers, and calling the Church Council at Nicaea (325) to settle issues of the faith. He was baptized only on the eve of his death in 337. Over the next century the pagan cults were destroyed, their priests deprived of support, their intellectuals bereft of standing.

So far as the Jews of the Land of Israel were concerned, not much changed at the Milvian Bridge in 312, when Constantine conquered in the sign of Christ. The sages' writings nowhere refer explicitly to that event. They scarcely gave testimony to its consequences for the Jews, and continued to harp upon prohibited relationships with "pagans" in general, as though nothing had changed from the third century to the fourth and fifth. Legal changes affecting the Jews under Constantine's rule indeed were not substantial. Jews could not proselytize; they could not circumcise slaves when they bought them; Jews could not punish other Jews who became Christians. Jews, finally, were required to serve on municipal councils wherever they lived, an onerous task involving responsibility for collecting taxes. But those who served synagogues, and patriarchs and priests, were still exempted from civil and personal obligations. In the reign of Constantius III (337—61), further laws aimed at separating Jews from Christians were enacted, in the Canons of Elvira of 339. These forbade intermarriage between Jews and Christians, further protected converts, and forbade Jews to hold slaves of Christian or other gentile origin.

The reversion to paganism on the part of the emperor Julian, ca. 360, brought a measure of favor to Jews and Judaism. To embarrass Christianity, he permitted the rebuilding of the Temple at Jerusalem. But he died before much progress could be made. In the aftermath of the fiasco of Julian's reversion to paganism, the Christians, returning to power, determined to make certain such a calamity would never recur. Accordingly, over the next century they undertook a sustained attack on the institutions and personnel of paganism in all its expressions. The long-term and systematic effort eventually overspread Judaism as well. From the accession of Theodosius II in 383 to the death of his son, Arcadius, in 408, Judaism came under attack. In the earlier part of the fifth century, Jews' rights and the standing of their corporate communities were substantially affected. The patriarchate of the Jews of the Land of Israel, the ethnarch and his administration, was abolished. So from the turn of the fifth century, the government policy meant to isolate Jews, lower their status, and suppress their agencies of self-rule.

Laws against intermarriage posed no problem to the Jews. The ones limiting proselytism and those protecting converts from Judaism did not affect many people. But the edicts that reduced Jews to second-class citizenship did matter. They were not to hold public office, but still had to sit on city councils responsible for the payment of taxes. Later, they were removed from the councils, though remaining obligated, of course, for taxes. Between 404 and 438 Jews were forbidden to hold office in the civil service, represent cities, serve in the army or at the bar, and ultimately were evicted from every public office. In all, the later fourth and fifth centuries for Israel in its land marked a time of significant change. Once a mere competing faith, Christianity now became paramount. The period from Julian's fall onward, moreover, presented to Israel problems of a profoundly religious character. To these we now turn.

There were five events of fundamental importance for the history of Judaism in the fourth and fifth centuries. All of them but the last were well-known in their own day. These were as follows: (1) the conversion of Constantine, (2) the fiasco of Julian's plan to rebuild the Temple of Jerusalem, (3) the depaganization of the Roman Empire, a program of attacks on pagan temples and, along the way, synagogues, (4) the Christianization of the majority of the population of Palestine, and (5) the creation of the Talmud of the Land of Israel and of compositions of scriptural exegeses. The Talmud and the exegetical compilations came into being in an age of high crisis, hope, and then disaster. Vast numbers of Jews now found chimerical the messianic expectation, as they had framed it around Julian's plan to rebuild the Temple. So it was a time of boundless expectations followed by bottomless despair.

Let us briefly review from the present perspective the four events that framed the setting for the fifth, starting with Constantine's conversion. The first point is that we do not know how Jews responded to Constantine's establishment of Christianity as the most favored religion. But in the Land of Israel itself his works were well-known, since he and his mother purchased many sites believed connected with Israel's sacred history and built churches and shrines at them. They rewrote the map of the Land of Israel. Every time they handled a coin, moreover, Jews had to recognize that something of fundamental importance had shifted, for the old pagan images were blotted out as Christian symbols took their place—public events indeed!

A move of the empire from reverence of Zeus to adoration of Mithra meant nothing; paganism was what it was, lacking all differentiation in the Jewish eye. Christianity was something else. It was different. It was like Judaism. Christians read the Torah and claimed to declare its meaning. Accordingly, the trend of sages' speculation cannot have avoided the issue of the place, within the Torah's messianic pattern, of the remarkable turn in world history represented by the triumph of Christianity. Since the Christians now celebrated confirmation of their faith in Christ's messiahship, and, at the moment, Jews were hardly prepared to concur, it falls surely within known patterns for us to suppose that Constantine's conversion would have been identified with some dark moment to prefigure the dawning of the messianic age.

If, second, people were then looking for a brief dawn, the emperor Julian's plan to rebuild the ruined Temple in Jerusalem must have dazzled their eyes. For while Constantine surely raised the messianic question, for a brief hour Emperor Julian appeared decisively to answer it. In 361 the now-pagan Julian gave permission to rebuild the Temple. Work briefly got underway, but stopped because of an earthquake. The intention of Julian's plan was quite explicit. Julian had had in mind to falsify the prophecy of Jesus that not one stone of the

Temple would be left upon another. We may take for granted that, since Christ's prophecy had not been proven false, many surely concluded that it indeed had now been shown true. We do not know that Jews in numbers drew the conclusion that, after all, Jesus really was the Christ. Many Christians said so. In the next half-century, Palestine gained a Christian majority. Christians were not slow to claim their faith had been proved right. We need not speculate on the depth of disappointment felt by those Jews who had hoped that the project would come to fruition and herald, instead of the Christian one, the Messiah they awaited.

Third, as we noted above, the last pagan emperor's threat to Christianity made urgent the delegitimization of paganism. The formation of a new and aggressive policy toward outsiders caught Judaism in the net too. To be sure, Jews were to be protected. But the sword unsheathed against the pagan cult places, if sharp, was untutored. It was not capable of discriminating among non-Christian centers of divine service. Nor could those who wielded it, zealots of the faith in church and street, have been expected to. The non-Christian Roman government protected synagogues and punished those who damaged them. Its policy was to extirpate paganism but protect a degraded Judaism. But the faithful of the church had their own ideas. The assault against pagan temples spilled over into an ongoing program of attacking synagogue property.

Still worse from the Jews' viewpoint, a phenomenon lacking much precedent over the antecedent thousand years now came into view: random attacks on Jews by reason of their faith, as distinct from organized struggles among contending and equal forces, Jewish and other mobs. The long-established Roman tradition of toleration of Judaism and of Jews, extending back to the time of Julius Caesar and applying both in law and in custom, now drew to a close. A new fact, at this time lacking all basis in custom and in the policy of state and Church alike, faced Jews: physical insecurity in their own villages and towns. So Jews' synagogues and their homes housed the same thing, which was to be eradicated: Judaism. A mark of exceptional piety came to consist in violence against Jews' holy places, their property and persons. Coming in the aftermath of the triumph of Christianity, on the one side, and the decisive disproof of the Jews' hope for the rebuilding of the Temple, on the other, was the hitherto-unimagined war against the Jews. In the last third of the fourth century and the beginning of the fifth, this war raised once again those questions about the meaning and end of history that Constantine, at the beginning of the age at hand, had forced upon Israel's consciousness.

Fourth, at this time there seems to have been a sharp rise in the numbers of Christians in the Holy Land. Christian refugees from the West accounted for part of the growth. But we have stories about how Jews converted as well. The number of Christian towns and villages dramatically increased. If Jews did convert in sizable numbers, then we should have to point to the events of the preceding decades as ample validation in their eyes for the Christian interpretation of history. Jews had waited nearly three hundred years, from the destruction in 70 C.E. to the promise of Julian. Instead of being falsified, Jesus' prophecy had been validated. No stone had been left on stone in the Temple, not after 70, not after 361, just as Jesus had said. Instead of a rebuilt Temple, the Jews looked out on a world in which now even their synagogues came under threat, and, along with them, their own homes and persons. What could be more ample proof of the truth of the Christians' claim than the worldly triumph of their Church? Resisted for so long, that claim called into question, as in the time of Bar Kokhba, whether it was worth waiting any longer for a messiah that had not come when he was most needed. With followers proclaiming the messiah who *had* come now possessing the world, the question could hardly be avoided.

No one may argue that, because a fair part of the population of the Land of Israel, possibly including numbers of Jews, evidently adopted Christianity after the conversion of Constantine, (particularly in the aftermath of the failure of Julian's plan to build the Temple, and the beginning of the Christian war against synagogue buildings and the start of chronic Jewish insecurity) the population that converted did so on account of the cumulative effect of these events. Why claim *post hoc, ergo propter hoc?* We merely observe a familiar pattern: (1) messianic hope, (2) post-messianic disillusion, (3) book. This pattern had played itself out two hundred years earlier, in the second century, the time of the Bar Kokhba war, messianic war, post-war disillusion, the Mishnah. Along these same lines, we notice in the later fourth and fifth centuries, (1) the messianic hope, aroused by Julian, (2) the deep disappointment consequent upon the failure to rebuild the Temple, and (3) the composition of both the Talmud of the Land of Israel and also important collections of scriptural exegeses, particularly including Genesis Rabbah, constructed of materials of essentially the same intellectual fabric. It is in this context that we interpret the formation of these fundamental documents of Judaism in the Land of Israel.

What were the tasks to be carried out through the writing of these books in behalf of, and within, the Jewish community, to which the framers addressed their work? First and foremost, there was the one brought to the forefront by the calamities of the later fourth and fifth centuries: apologetics. Whether or not the Christians now pointed to historical events as proof that Jesus indeed had been Christ, and that Israel-after-the-flesh had been punished for rejecting him as the Messiah, we do not know. These messages to be sure were standard. But we cannot demonstrate that, in just three decades. Jews paid attention to them. Still, they did not have to turn to Christian critics to tell them what they surely recognized on their own. Israel's condition in its own land proved ever more parlous. The status of "the Torah" declined, and, with it, the standing and security of Israel. Whatever the world may have said, Jews themselves surely had to wonder whether history was headed in the right direction, and whether indeed the Christians, emerging from within Israel itself, may not initially have been right. For the Roman Empire now was Christian. Israel's most recent bout with the messianic fever had proved disastrous. Julian's Temple had not been built. If, as is surely likely, some Jews thought that the building of that Temple would mean the Messiah was near at hand—or in fact had come—then the failure to build the Temple meant the Messiah was not near, or never would come in the way Jews expected. The requirement to construct an apologetics therefore emerged from the condition of Israel, whether or not, in addition, Christian polemicists had a hearing among Jews.

If, now, we inquire into what in fact sages did at that time, the answer is clear. They composed the Talmud of the Land of Israel as we know it. They collected exegeses of Scripture and made them into systematic and sustained accounts of, initially, the meaning of the Pentateuch (assuming dates in these centuries for Sifra, the two Sifrés, Genesis Rabbah and Leviticus Rabbah). So on the face of it we have to ask about the utility, for the large apologetic exercise, of the editorial work done at that time.

When we recall what Christians had to say to Israel, we may find entirely reasonable the view that compiling scriptural exegeses constituted part of a Jewish apologetic response. For one Christian mes-

sage had been that Israel "after the flesh" had distorted and continually misunderstood the meaning of what had been its own Scripture. Failing to read the Old Testament in the light of the New, the
prophetic promises in the perspective of Christ's fulfillment of those
promises, Israel "after the flesh" had lost access to God's revelation to
Moses at Sinai. If we were to propose a suitably powerful, yet appropriately proud, response, it would have two qualities. First, it would
supply a complete account of what Scripture had meant, and always
must mean, as Israel read it. Second, it would do so in such a way as
not to dignify the position of the other side with the grace of an
explicit reply at all.

The compilations of exegeses accomplished at this time assuredly
take up the challenge of restating the meaning of the Torah revealed
by God to Moses at Mount Sinai. This the sages did in a systematic and
thorough way. At the same time, if the charges of the other side
precipitated the work of compilation and composition, the consequent collections in no way suggest so. The issues of the documents
are made always to emerge from the inner life not even of Israel in
general, but of the sages' estate in particular. Scripture was thor-
oughly rabbinized, as earlier it had been Christianized. None of this
suggests the other side had won a response for itself. Only the net
effect—a complete picture of the whole, as Israel must perceive the
whole of revelation—suggests the extraordinary utility for apologetics, outside as much as inside the faith, served by these same
compilations. And that utility is discerned only by us, long after the
fact and only in general.

In this same context we also observe that the rabbis' insistence on
the authority of traditions in addition to Scripture, laws contained
then in the Mishnah and whatever other documents sages treasured,
had long provoked a further polemic. The other side held that Israel
not only could not read and understand the ancient revelation of God
to Moses at Mount Sinai. Israel furthermore had changed and falsified
that revelation. This was by adding things not in the Old Testament
or by changing the substance of the law through appeal to other
sources of truth than Sinai. A ready answer to this critique, surely
deriving from within Israel, emerged from the systematic provision
of biblical proof-texts for the Mishnah. To claim that people looked
for proof-texts for the Mishnah in order to know what to answer the
other side is excessive. Ample motivation for undertaking the same

search was simply that Jews, as much as outsiders within the larger scriptural commonwealth, were asking the same questions. So in doing what they did for the Mishnah, sages indeed provided a suitable reply, at least for themselves.

A still more powerful apologetic for Judaism emerged from the implicit conviction, everywhere present and always taken for granted in sages' writings, that things in ancient times were precisely as they had emerged in the life of present-day Israel. The insistence of all compilations of scriptural exegeses as much as of the Talmud was that ancient Israel had always lived in accord with the rabbis' vision of Israel. The innocent anachronism, projecting backward patterns of belief and behavior of sages' own world and time, of course is to be expected. Any other conception in context was unthinkable. But the uses of anachronism are many. One important instance, in the present argument, as we shall see, turns out to be the identification of David, in particular, as a rabbi and as the model for the rabbis of the later age as well. But David was also the Messiah's progenitor, so the Messiah would be like a rabbi. Given the crisis of faith precipitated by the triumph of Christianity and the disappointment of the messianic hope of Judaism, we may hardly wonder at the uses to which this particular expression of the prevailing anachronism might be put in the salvific debates of the age.

The framers of both the Talmud and collections of scriptural exegeses naturally took for granted that the world they knew in the fourth and fifth centuries had flourished a thousand and more years earlier. The values they embodied and the supernatural powers they fantasized for themselves were predictably projected backward onto biblical figures. The ubiquitous citation of biblical proof-texts in support of both legal and theological statements shows the mentality of the sages. In their imagination, everything they said stood in direct continuity with what Scripture had stated. Biblical and rabbinical authorities lived on a single plane of being, in a single age of shared discourse.

Now to proceed to interpret the matter at hand, we have to step aside for a moment and review the point of emphasis of the Mishnah's system. Only then do we see the transformation effected over two hundred years. The Mishnah had presented a system of sanctification. Its emphasis lay upon the creation of a world of order and stability, perfected as the world had been at the moment of its original creation. When the world was wholly in place, then, as when God had made the world, God would finish the world and sanctify it. Now when we address the questions of Messiah, the meaning and end of history, the rescue of Israel from its political circumstance, we deal not with *sanctification* but with the *salvation* of Israel—a different dimension of being and of meaning altogether. Sanctification constitutes a category of ontology; salvation, an issue of eschatology and so of ongoing history. To be holy is to *be*. To be saved is to be saved *from* something and *for* something. The language of the Mishnah is a language of holiness, and the language at hand, with its interest in events and their meaning, with history and eschatology, is a language of salvation. So we have to recognize that the issues, at least as I attempt to outline them, testify to a massive shift, from a system of stasis and sanctification, with slight interest in historical events, to a system of movement toward salvation, with intense attention to what was happening.

If, then, we speak no longer of sanctification but rather of salvation, we now recognize what has changed. Exegesis of Scripture, with attention to the particular, messianic (David) passages at hand, signals a shift in the depths of sages' conception of what is important. That is why what is consequential in this emphasis upon (to us) anachronistic exegesis is the theory of salvation thereby given its clearest statement. What was the rabbis' view of salvation? Seeing Scripture in their own model, they took the position that the Torah of old, its supernatural power and salvific promise, in their own day continued to endure among themselves. In consequence, the promise of salvation contained in every line of Scripture was to be kept in every deed of learning and obedience to the law effected under their auspices. To be sure they projected backward the things they cherished in an act of (to us) extraordinary anachronism. But in their eyes they carried forward, to their own time, and themselves embodied the promise of salvation for Israel contained within the written Torah of old.

In this aspect the mode of thought and the consequent salvific proposition conformed to the model revealed likewise in the Gospel of Matthew. The reason Scripture was cited, for both statements on Israel's salvation—that of Matthew, that of the exegetical compositions—was not to establish or validate authority alone. Rather, it was to identify what was happening at just that time with what had happened long ago. The purpose then was not merely to demonstrate and authenticate the bona fide character of a new figure of salvation. It was to show the continuity of the salvific process. The point is that the figure at hand was not new at all. He stood as a renewed exemplar and avatar of Israel's eternal hope, now come to full realization—a very different thing. Authenticity hardly demanded demonstration of scriptural origin. That was the datum of the more extreme claim laid down in the profoundly anachronistic reading accorded to Scripture. In finding *sages* in the (written) Torah, therefore, the sages of the exegetical compositions and the Talmud implicitly stated a view of themselves as the continuation and model of the sanctified way of life of the written Torah. It followed that the pattern and promise of salvation contained therein found full embodiment in their teachings and way of life. That is the meaning of the explicit reading of the present into the past. It is the implicit arrogation of the hope of the past to the salvific heroes of the present: themselves.

Who can imagine, therefore, a more powerful apologetic to offer the disappointed, indeed despairing community of Israel than the simple one contained in the sages' systematic reading and exposition of the meaning of the ancient Scriptures of Israel? To be sure, we do not know who listened to the apologetic. But the Jewish nation indeed continued in its land down to the Sasanian Persian and later Arab conquests and beyond. The nation took an active part in the wars of the early seventh century; it remained numerous and effective. So someone must have heard the sages' message, or the nation surely would have disintegrated and amalgamated into the new Israel, now everywhere triumphant.

The labor of exegesis takes on still more concrete interest when we make explicit the salvific message contained within the method itself, I mean, the methodical reading of the old in terms of the new life of Israel, the Jewish nation. To state matters simply, if Moses, "our rabbi," and David, King of Israel, were (as sages everywhere claimed) like a rabbi today, then a rabbi today stood as successor to the throne of Moses, our rabbi, and could reveal God's will. A rabbi today could be the son of David who was to come as King of Israel. It is not surprising, therefore, that among the many biblical heroes whom the rabbis treated as sages, principal and foremost was Moses, treated as the model of the rabbi, and David, made into a messianic rabbi or a rabbinical Messiah. David as the sage of the Torah served as avatar and model for the sages of their own time. That view was made explicit in detail. If, for instance, a rabbi was jealous to have his traditions cited in his own name, it was because that was David's stated view as well. In more general terms, both David and Moses are represented as students of Torah, just like the disciples and sages of the current time. Here is one minor example.

> Y. Sanhedrin 2:6. [IV.A] It is written, "And David said longingly, 'O that someone would give me water to drink from the well of Bethlehem [which is by the gate]'" (1 Chron. 11:17).
> [B] R. Hiyya bar Ba said, "He required a teaching of law."
> [C] "Then the three mighty men broke through [the camp of the Philistines]" (1 Chron. 11:18).
> [D] Why three? Because the law is not decisively laid down by fewer than three.

The triviality of the foregoing instance of the rabbinization of scriptural heroes, including David himself, should underline the larger importance of the process. It is simply taken for granted that David was a rabbi. If he wanted water, it could only mean, the "water of the Torah." If he sent three soldiers, it was because three judges were needed. So the military tale is turned into a Torah story. Every detail of the verses of Scripture is read in the light of a totally alien program.

This sort of rereading of Scripture encompassed a vast number of passages. What is important for our argument is that, in particular, Moses and David were turned into principal rabbis and models for the rabbis of the new age. No one could miss the deep meaning. Through representing Moses, David, and other biblical heroes as they did, the framers of the exegetical compilations and of the Talmud provided a considerable body of evidence of Israel's continuing hope. For, through the labor of exegesis of Mishnah and Scripture alike, sages themselves turned out to do those very things that the ancient, and coming, saviors of Israel had done, and would again do in time to come. Moses and David in the long-ago past and in the age to come, and sages here and now—all formed part of the supernatural basis for the single, certain hope for Israel. In this context, the framing of exegeses of Scriptures and the collection of such exegeses into holy books constituted an act heavy with salvific meaning and promise.

We note, finally, one further aspect of the utility of the resort to exegesis of Scripture in the apologetic venture. In addition to endemic anachronism, we observe something far more accessible, both then and now, to us as outsiders to the rabbinic system: a concern for the close and careful explanation of words and phrases. We may well be struck by the interest in the mere facts of the meaning of words and phrases, proved by perfectly reasonable resort to data made available by other words and phrases, the meaning of which was already known. The very facticity of discourse should not be missed. It too bears meaning. For the numerous passages in the collections of exegeses in which theological exegeses—through apologetics, dogmatics, mere homiletics, or historical anachronism—dominate are outweighed by the still more numerous ones of a different sort. In these more common exegeses there is a clear claim that any reasonable and informed person must read things in this way and not in some other. What is particular to the rabbinic perspective thus competes with what may prove acceptable to outsiders as well.

The apologetic use of this second sort of reading of the ancient verses of Scripture, the one we may characterize as philological or, at least, other-than-theological, is now to be specified. It makes possible a second sort of discourse. If the theological passage is to address the insider, the philological kind (in the mind of the insider at least) speaks to the world at large. This other, general mode of discourse about Scripture serves to persuade the insider that outsiders, reasonable and informed people, may well accept what the exegete has to say. A powerful apologetic—addressed, self-evidently, to the believer—thereby emerges. What we say about Scripture's meanings is reasonable and demonstrable, not merely to be believed by a private act of faith. It is to be critically examined, assented to by shared reason. So the claim of the exegete to provide mere facts supplies the most powerful apologetic. Transforming convictions into (mere) facts serves to reenforce the faith of the believer, beyond all argument from revelation, let alone historical confirmation. How better to do this than work out exegeses serving to clarify, demonstrating through the appeal to self-evident proofs and incontrovertible data of language.

To whom is such exegesis serviceable in apologetics? The appeal to the plain meaning of Scripture and how it coincides with the particular position, on the meaning of Scripture, taken by the apologist, serves in particular not the dominant but the subordinate party to the debate. The winning side may rearrange things, appropriate proof for their convictions as compelling as the very topography of the land

and geography of the world. What better proof did Christianity's exponents have to offer than the argument from history? Look at any coin, with its Christian symbol, and the facts come clear. Everything Christ had said was proved true. Reconstructing the geography of the Holy Land made the same point. Anything Israel (after the flesh) had hoped to see had turned out ashes and dust. Lacking access to, unable to change, the facts of reality, the rabbinical apologists through their approach to the reading of Scripture could appeal only to the facts of revelation, as (rightly) construed by them. These too, in the nature of things, constituted facts. They were, moreover, the only palatable facts left for the subordinate side.

A glance backward at the way in which Aphrahat, sage of the oppressed Christian Church of Iranian Babylonia not even a century earlier, had conducted his debate with the dominant Judaism of his locale provides a striking parallel. Writing ca. 330, during a time of severe Iranian persecution of Christianity, Aphrahat addressed the Jewish critics of the Church. If their arguments tempted the faithful, the Jews who pointed to the calamity affecting Christianity as evidence of the falsity of the claim of Christ to be Messiah only said out loud what some within the Church were thinking. Aphrahat's mode of argument took the form of a stunningly reasonable reading of the shared statements—facts—of Scripture. He adduced the scriptural facts, on which all parties agreed, to prove that, despite the events of the hour, the Christians, not the Jews, truly understood and lived by the faith of Sinai. Appeal to facts shared by all parties, the claim to speak in accord with the canons of reason universally compelling for every side—these serve in particular the polemical requirements of the weak. The strong define logic for themselves and declare what is reasonable.

I need hardly point out that this perspective on the compilations of scriptural exegeses composed in the trying times of the fifth and sixth centuries is gained only by viewing them from very far away. It is not only *post facto*. Comparing two different sources of exegeses—Aphrahat's and the sages'—centered on establishing facts and finding shared bases for difference is a very general argument indeed. Still, when we consider that, from the fifth century onward, Jewish participants in the Jewish-Christian argument invariably conducted the debate through reference to Scripture, its language and facts, normally avoiding the confrontation with the miserable condition of

Israel in contrast to the triumphant success of Christianity, the comparison becomes compelling. For it is a commonplace to observe that the institutions of the fourth, fifth, and sixth centuries form the bridge from Middle Eastern antiquity to the medieval, hence modern, West. To that commonplace, I may add the suggestion that the main outlines of the Jewish-Christian argument of medieval and early modern times may be discerned in the form of the scriptural studies taken by the fifth- and sixth-century sages. These were (1) close reading of verses of the Scripture, (2) composition of exegeses into large collections, (3) all the time pretending to no apologetic motive, but (4) claiming only to say what things really meant.

That was, and would remain, the Jewish position, because, in the nature of things, the Jews, being weak, would always resort to the weapons of the weak: denial of the strength of the strong through exaggeration of the power of (shared) reason to coerce the strong to accommodate the weak. That position emerges less in the detail of what was said about Scripture than from two simple facts: first, how much was said about Scripture, and, second, how much effort would go into compiling and preserving what was said as a statement of what God had said, of what therefore was so.

12

Revelation, Canon, and Scriptural Authority: (2) The Theological Context

The crisis for Judaism presented by the political triumph of Christianity cannot define the context or generative considerations in which the exegetical documents came to formation. Nor may we claim that the documents were held authoritative within Judaism merely because we see in them the utility of having something to say to the wavering faithful. The exegetical documents were composed of statements on the meaning of Scripture. Where did these statements come from? Were they revealed? The framers of the documents collected and presented as authoritative books these sets of statements on the meaning of Scripture. What status then did the composers of the collections claim for their books? Were they *torah* (revelation) and part of the Torah? Accordingly, both the contents of the compilations of scriptural exegeses and the collections themselves make necessary an inquiry into the complementary contexts of a theological and canonical character, in which *midrash* as a mode of writing and of compiling a holy book took place. Let me now unpack the two questions at hand.

When a sage had framed an opinion on the meaning of a verse, whether supplying a close exegesis or constructing a wide-ranging discourse, and that sage, or others, had collected numerous exegeses and strung them together into a collection, the status of the book surely had to be determined. Clearly, the authors or compilers claimed to state the meaning of Scripture. Was that book of imputed meanings—exegeses—held to be the same as Scripture, that is, a book of *torah* or revelation? The collection contained statements of the Torah, that is, citations of Pentateuchal writings, as well as authoritative judgments on the meanings of those statements. As such, the author, or the people who received the work and venerated it, may have regarded the whole as equivalent to the Torah. On the other hand, people knew the difference between the text of Scripture, written down in a sacred scroll, and what authorities of their own day and age had to say about the meaning of the text. Did the distinction between media make a difference? The issue of the relationship between collections of exegeses of Scripture and Scripture itself requires attention. The latter was revealed. What was the source of the former? The latter enjoyed the status of the word and will of God for Israel. Why pay attention to the former? At issue was the standing of the sage who made up the exegeses and collected them.

The source and authority of the compilations of biblical exegeses—revealed by God along with the Scripture subjected to exegesis, or made up by men and in no way part of revelation—furthermore governed the complementary question of the status and authority of the collections of exegeses in relationship to the established "canon" of the Hebrew Scriptures—if there really was one. On the one side, if people conceded that the collections of exegeses derived from God's word and expressed God's meaning in Scripture, then the compositions of exegeses demanded a place within the canon of authoritative sacred writings of Israel. On the other, if the collections of exegeses preserved the opinions of ordinary men, albeit sages of exceptional learning, then the canon need not open up to accommodate them. The issue of the source and authority of the exegeses, hence of the compositions made up of them, drew in its wake the closely related question of the place and standing of the documents that contained and preserved these exegetical writings. Once more, the heart of the matter was the standing of the sage.

The compilations before us present no answers to the questions at hand. Like other rabbinic documents, they do their business with remarkably little explanation implying self-consciousness. Within the bounds of the document itself, no effort goes into identifying the author and his authority, defining the nature of the work and its purpose, indicating the prospective audience for discourse and its desired response. Obviously, to the framers of the collections, the answers to these questions must have been obvious. But they do not

tell us what they were. The reason, I think, is that all rabbinic documents came to fullness within an established matrix of mind and
imagination. Since everyone engaged in the work of formation and
composition knew the meaning of the creation of any document, no
one found it necessary to explain what he was doing. That is why,
after the Mishnah itself, no document of formative Judaism—the
writings of sages from the second through the seventh centuries—
contains a full and complete account of itself, its context and intent.
Except for the Mishnah, all rabbinic writings form fragments of a
complete system, itself nowhere fully exposed in a single document.

What then defines that matrix into which the collections of exegeses of Scripture were born, and to the configuration of which they
too give evidence? Since these collections point elsewhere, they
depend upon facts outside of their own compositions for definition of
what is collected within them. We turn forthwith to the ubiquitous
figure everywhere in the wings. We now call to center-stage him who
speaks in these collections: the rabbi himself. The issues of the status
of the exegeses of Scripture collected in the documents at hand, of the
relationship of the collections themselves to the "established canon,"
and of revelation after Scripture—these are to be resolved only when
we know the status, in Heaven and on earth, and the standing, in the
context of Torah, of the sage.

No rabbinic document presents a complete account of the system of
rabbinic Judaism, and every rabbinic document presupposes a fully
developed system. But if no book tells us how to grasp the system as a
whole, then where shall we find it? The obvious locus for the dis-
covery of the encompassing and definitive category, within which all
else will find proper location and definition, surely lies in the name by
which we call the thing itself. Since we speak of rabbinic Judaism, we
have ample reason to turn to the figure of the rabbi. In that figure we
should find the center of gravity, the force that holds the whole
together. In the authority of the rabbi we should uncover warrant for
the inclusion of the compilations of exegeses of Scripture into the
Torah's canon. In the supernatural standing of the rabbi, we should
perceive grounds for regarding the exegeses themselves as *torah*,
revelation, within the Torah.

If, in the figure of the rabbi as he emerges in diverse rabbinic texts,
we do not uncover answers to the questions about the status and
authority of things rabbis wrote, we are not apt to find out elsewhere.

For, as I said, the texts themselves presuppose that everyone knows what, in fact, lies wholly beyond demonstration within the body of any one of the various texts. All we have as fact is that rabbis claimed to enjoy full authority to declare the meaning of both Scripture and the Mishnah. This they did in massive and authoritative works, of *midrash* and Talmud alike. What we want to ask then is whether sages held God had told them what to say in these writings. If so, did they claim their books consequently belonged to the Torah? When we know who and what the rabbi said he was, we also shall turn up clear responses to the issues of revelation and canon as I just now suggested that these pertain to collections of scriptural exegeses.

The strategy of argument requires that we repeat the simple exercise on which this entire account of the context of *midrash* rests: taxonomy. We compare what people did in one, known context with what they did in another, unknown one. So we establish lines of comparison and contrast from the one to the other, applying to the unknown the facts revealed by the known. We have now to repeat the same procedure. For we do know how, in the Talmud, the rabbis related what they had to say about their authority vis-à-vis the two sources of truth in their hands, the Scripture and the Mishnah. Accordingly, when we see how, in the Talmud, the rabbis treated their own views in the setting of the exegesis of the Mishnah and Scripture alike, we shall understand the status they likely accorded to their exegeses of Scripture. At that point we shall have whatever answer we are apt to find, generated solely within the limits of the documents in hand, to the questions raised in the preceding sections.

Once more, therefore, a simple equation, now established as fact, guides us: the Talmud is to the Mishnah as the collections of scriptural exegeses are to Scripture. Hence, when we know the status in the Talmud of rabbinical statements about the Mishnah and about Scripture, we shall reach proper conclusions about the status accorded to those same statements in the compilations of scriptural exegeses.

Let me state the result at the outset. Sages' talmudic statements about the Mishnah are treated precisely as are statements found both *in* the Mishnah and *in* Scripture itself. Thus, talmudic statements either form part of *torah*, or are wholly derivative from the Torah and hence of the same status and standing as Torah. Likewise, statements in the compositions of scriptural exegeses about the meaning of Scripture, and, by extension, the collections themselves enjoy the status of revelation and form part of the canon of Torah, of Judaism. The upshot is that what the rabbi says is *torah*. The collections of exegeses were received in revelation and belong in the canon as part of the Torah.

Let us now examine in a few examples exactly how the Talmud proposes to analyze opinions of its own authorities, the rabbis of the third and fourth centuries themselves. Then the preceding statements will find ample justification in sources.

We began our inquiry by pointing out that a principal mode of the exegesis of the Mishnah was to supply proof-texts for the Mishnah's various statements. This served to link what the Mishnah said to principles and rules of Scripture. What we shall now again observe, through a single interesting instance, is that the same inquiry pertaining to the Mishnah applies without variation to statements made by rabbis of the contemporary period themselves. Indeed, precisely the same theological and exegetical considerations came to bear upon both the Mishnah's statements and opinions expressed by Talmudic rabbis. Since these were not to be distinguished from one another in the requirement that opinion be suitably grounded in Scripture, they also should be understood to have formed part of precisely the same corpus of (scriptural) truths. What the Mishnah and the later rabbi said further expressed precisely the same kind of truth: revelation, through the medium of Scripture, whether contained in the Mishnah or in the opinion of the sage himself. While this matter is familiar from our interest in the role of Scripture in the exegesis of the Mishnah, we review it to establish the main point of the argument: the context in which all exegesis took place, the polemic which, by indirection, exegesis served.

The way in which this search for proof-texts applies equally to the Mishnah and to the rabbi's opinion is illustrated in the following passage.

Yerushalmi Sanhedrin 10:4: [A] *The party of Korah has no portion in the world to come, and will not live in the world to come [Mishnah Sanhedrin 10:4].*

[B] What is the Scriptural basis for this view?

[C] "So they and all that belonged to them went down alive into Sheol; and the earth closed over them, and they perished from the midst of the assembly" (Num. 16:33).

[D] *"The earth closed over them"—in this world.*

[E] *"And they perished from the midst of the assembly"* — *in the world to come [Mishnah Sanhedrin 10:4D–F].*

[F] It was taught: R. Judah b. Batera says, "The contrary view is to be derived from the implication of the following verse:

[G] "'I have gone astray like a lost sheep; seek thy servant and do not forget thy commandments' (Ps. 119:176).

[H] "Just as the lost object which is mentioned later on in the end is going to be searched for, so the lost object which is stated herein is destined to be searched for" [Tosefta Sanhedrin 13:9].

[I] Who will pray for them?

[J] R. Samuel bar Nahman said, "Moses will pray for them.

[K] [This is proved from the following verse:] "'Let Reuben live, and not die, [nor let his men be few]' (Deut. 33:6)."

[L] R. Joshua b. Levi said, "Hannah will pray for them."

[M] This is the view of R. Joshua b. Levi, for R. Joshua b. Levi said, "Thus did the party of Korah sink ever downward, until Hannah went and prayed for them and said, 'The Lord kills and brings to life; he brings down to Sheol and raises up' (1 Sam. 2:6)."

We have a striking sequence of proof-texts, serving (1) the cited statement of the Mishnah, A–C, then (2) an opinion of a rabbi in the Tosefta, F–H, then (3) the position of a rabbi, J–K, L–M. The process of providing proof-texts therefore is central, the nature of the passages requiring the proof-texts a matter of indifference. We see that the search for appropriate verses of Scripture vastly transcends the purpose of study of the Mishnah and Scripture, exegesis of their rules, or provision of adequate authority for the Mishnah and its laws. In fact, any proposition that is to be taken seriously, whether in the Mishnah, in the Tosefta, or in the mouth of a Talmudic sage himself, will elicit interest in scriptural support.

This quest in Scripture thus extended beyond the interest in supplying the Mishnah's rules with proof-texts. On the contrary, the real issue turns out to have been not the Mishnah at all, nor even the vindication of its diverse sayings, one by one. Once the words of a *sage*, not merely a rule of the Mishnah, are made to refer to Scripture for proof, it must follow that, in the natural course of things, a rule of the Mishnah or of the Tosefta will likewise be asked to refer to Scripture. The fact that the living sage validated his own words through Scripture explains why the sage in the fourth century validated also the words of the (then) ancient sages of the Mishnah and Tosefta through verses of Scripture. It is one, undivided phenomenon.

Distinctions are not made among media—oral, written, living, book
—of *torah.*

We turn to the way in which the rabbis of the Talmud proposed to
resolve differences of opinion. This is important, because the Mishnah
presents a mass of disputes. Turning speculation about principles into
practical law required resolving them. Precisely in the same way in
which talmudic rabbis settled disputes in the Mishnah and so attained
a consensus about the law of the Mishnah, they handled disputes
among themselves. The importance of that fact for our argument is
simple. Once more we see that the rabbis of the third and fourth
centuries, represented in the Talmud, treated their own contem-
poraries exactly as they treated the then-ancient authorities of the
Mishnah. In their minds the status accorded to the Mishnah, as a
derivative of the Torah, applies equally to the talmudic sages' teachings. In the following instance we see how the same discourse
attached to (1) a Mishnah rule is assigned as well to one in (2) the
Tosefta and, at the end, to differences among (3) the talmudic authorities.

> *Yerushalmi Ketubot 5:1:* [VI.A] R. Jacob bar Aha, R. Alexa in the
> name of Hezekiah: "The law accords with the view of R. Eleazar b.
> Azariah, who stated, *If she was widowed or divorced at the stage of
> betrothal, the virgin collects only two hundred zuz and the widow, a
> maneh. If she was widowed or divorced at the stage of a consummated
> marriage, she collects the full amount [M. Ket. 5:1E, D]."*
>
> [B] R. Hananiah said, "The law accords with the view of R. Eleazar b.
> Azariah."
>
> [C] Said Abayye, "They said to R. Hananiah, 'Go and shout [outside
> whatever opinion you like.' But] R. Jonah, R. Zeira in the name of R.
> Jonathan said, 'The law accords with the view of R. Eleazar b. Azariah.'
> [Yet] R. Yosa bar Zeira in the name of R. Jonathan said, 'The law does
> not accord with the view of R. Eleazar b. Azariah.' [So we do not in fact
> know the decision.]"
>
> [D] Said R. Yose, "We had a mnemonic. Hezekiah and R. Jonathan both
> say one thing."
>
> [E] For it has been taught:
>
> [F] He whose son went abroad, and whom they told, "Your son has
> died,"
>
> [G] and who went and wrote over all his property to someone else as a
> gift,
>
> [H] and whom they afterward informed that his son was yet alive—

[I] his deed of gift remains valid.

[J] R. Simeon b. Menassia says, "His deed of gift is not valid, for if he had known that his son was alive, he would never have made such a gift" [T. Ket. 4:14E–H].

[K] Now R. Jacob bar Aha [= A] said, "The law is in accord with the view of R. Eleazar b. Azariah, and the opinion of R. Eleazar b. Azariah is the same in essence as that of R. Simeon b. Menassia."

[L] Now R. Yannai said to R. Hananiah, "Go and shout [outside whatever you want].

[M] "But, said R. Yose bar Zeira in the name of R. Jonathan, 'The law is not in accord with R. Eleazar b. Azariah.'"

[N] But in fact the case was to be decided in accord with the view of R. Eleazar b. Azariah.

What is important here is that the Talmud makes no distinction whatever when deciding the law of disputes (1) in the Mishnah, (2) in the Tosefta, and (3) among talmudic rabbis. The same already-formed colloquy that is applied at the outset to the Mishnah's dispute is then held equally applicable to the Tosefta's. The process of thought is the main thing, without regard to the document to which the process applies.

Still more important than the persistence of a given mode of thought applicable to Scripture, to the Mishnah, and to the sayings of talmudic rabbis themselves is the presentation of the rabbi as a law-giver in the model of Moses. The capacity of the sage himself to participate in the process of revelation is illustrated in two types of materials. First of all, tales told about rabbis' behavior on specific occasions immediately were translated into rules for the entire community to keep. Accordingly, he was a source not merely of good example but of prescriptive law:

> Y. *Abodah Zarah* 5:4: [III.X] R. Aha went to Emmaus, and he ate dumpling [prepared by Samaritans].
>
> [Y] R. Jeremiah ate leavened bread prepared by them.
>
> [Z] R. Hezekiah ate their locusts prepared by them.
>
> [AA] R. Abbahu prohibited Israelite use of wine prepared by them.

These reports of what rabbis had done enjoyed the same authority as statements of the law on eating what Samaritans cooked, as did citations of traditions in the names of the great authorities of old. What someone did served as a norm, if he was a sage of sufficient standing.

Second, and far more common, are instances in which the deed of a rabbi is adduced as an authoritative precedent for the law under discussion. It was everywhere taken for granted that what a rabbi did he did because of his mastery of the law. Even though a formulation of the law was not in hand, a tale about what a rabbi actually did constituted adequate evidence on how to formulate the law itself. So on the basis of the action or practice of an authority, a law might be framed that was quite independent of the person of the sage. The sage then functioned as a lawgiver, like Moses. Among many instances of that mode of generating law are the following:

Y. *Abodah Zarah 3:11:* [II.A] Gamaliel Zuga was walking along, leaning on the shoulder of R. Simeon b. Laqish. They came across an image.
[B] He said to him, "What is the law as to passing before it?"
[C] He said to him, "Pass before it, but close [your] eyes."
[D] R. Isaac was walking along, leaning on the shoulder of R. Yohanan. They came across an idol before the council building.
[E] He said to him, "What is the law as to passing before it?"
[F] He said to him, "Pass before it, but close [your] eyes."
[G] R. Jacob bar Idi was walking along, leaning upon R. Joshua b. Levi. They came across a procession in which an idol was carried. He said to him, "Nahum, the most holy man, passed before this idol, and will you not pass by it? Pass before it but close your eyes."

Y. *Abodah Zarah 2:2:* [III.FF] R. Aha had chills and fever. [They brought him] a medicinal drink prepared from the phallus of Dionysian revelers [thus Jastrow, I 400 B]. But he would not drink it. They brought it to R. Jonah, and he did drink it. Said R. Mana, "Now if R. Jonah, the patriarch, had known what it was, he would never have drunk it."
[GG] Said R. Huna, "That is to say, 'They do not accept healing from something that derives from an act of fornication.'"

The point of these stories requires no repetition. What is important is GG, the rewording of the point of the story as a law. Since the purpose of this exercise is clear, let us proceed directly to the conclusions to be drawn from it.

Having come this far, we must now wonder whether, any longer, we can distinguish between *torah*, as divine revelation, and "the canon of the Torah," a particular set of books deemed more authoritative than any other books. If what an authorized rabbi states must be received as *torah*, as divine revelation, then we face two possibilities. Either there is *torah* which is not part of the Torah, the canon of revelation. Or there is no such thing as a canon at all. That is to say, the conception that, at a given point, a particular set of books is declared to be the final and authoritative statement of God's will and word, in the present context seems to me puzzling. The entire thrust of the exegetical process is to link upon a single plane of authority and reliability what a rabbi now says with what the (written) Torah said, what the Mishnah says with what the (written) Torah said, or what the Tosefta says with what the (written) Torah said.

What that means is simple. The sages of the Talmud recognized no distinction in authority or standing—hence, in status as revelation—between what the Mishnah said and what the written Torah said. They also used the same processes of validation to demonstrate that what they themselves declared enjoyed the same standing and authority as what they found in the written Torah. So their intent always was to show there in fact were no gradations in revelation. God spoke in various ways and through diverse media: to prophets and to sages, in writing and in memorized sayings, to olden times and to the present day. We can discern no systematic effort to distinguish one kind of revelation from another—revelation transmitted in writing, that transmitted orally, revelation to an ancient prophet, an exegesis or a Torah-teaching of a contemporary sage. Then it must follow, as I now propose, that sages rejected the conception of layers and levels of revelations, of making distinctions between one medium and another, hence one book and another.

To state matters simply: either a teaching was true and authoritative, wherever it was found and however it had reached the living age, or a teaching was untrue and not authoritative. Scripture, the Mishnah, the sage—all three spoke with equal authority. True, one thing had to come into alignment with the other, the Mishnah with Scripture, the sage with the Mishnah. But it was not the case that one component of *torah*, of God's word to Israel, stood within the sacred circle, another beyond. Interpretation and what was interpreted, exegesis and text, belonged together. In so vivid a world of divine address, what place was there for the conception of canon? There was none. And how can we show the distinction between canonical and non-canonical? We cannot. The truth as God declared it was canon. Everything else was not. So, to conclude, the conception of canon contradicts the theory of *torah* revealed in the Talmud of the Land of Israel and in the earliest collections of biblical exegeses.

Scripture and the Mishnah govern what the rabbi knows. But it is *the rabbi* who authoritatively speaks about them. The simple fact is that what rabbis were willing to do to the Mishnah is precisely what they were prepared to do to Scripture—impose upon it their own judgment of its meaning. This fact is the upshot of the inquiry now completed. It also is the sole fact we have in hand for the identification of the context of *midrash* in formative Judaism. But it suffices. Since we see that the question of locus and setting devolves upon several books at once—Scripture and the Mishnah equally, so far as the Talmud is concerned—the answer to the question of context must come from something other than a book or even a set of books. It is the source of the authority of the rabbi himself that turns out to pose the fundamental question. With the answer to that question, we also know, first, the status, as to revelation, of the things the rabbi says, whether he speaks of the Mishnah or of Scripture; and second, the standing of the books he writes, whether these are tractates of the Talmud or the compositions of exegeses of Scripture.

The reason why the collections of scriptural exegeses do not contain answers to our questions of their theological and canonical status is that these questions, in their setting, were impertinent. These questions had been answered before the books came to be written. The books could not have been written the way they were if the questions at hand had not been answered in a particular way and in a prior setting. So everything turns upon the figure of the rabbi.

The rabbi speaks with authority about the Mishnah and the Scripture. He therefore has authority deriving from revelation. He himself may participate in the processes of revelation (there is no material difference). Since that is so, the rabbi's book, whether Talmud to the Mishnah or *midrash* to Scripture, is *torah*, that is, revealed by God. It also forms part of the Torah, a fully "canonical" document. The reason, then, is that the rabbi is like Moses, "our rabbi," who received *torah* and wrote the Torah.

Since rabbinical documents repeatedly claim that, if you want to know the law, you should not only listen to what the rabbi says but also copy what he does, it follows that, in his person, the rabbi represents and embodies the Torah. God in the Torah revealed God's will and purpose for the world. So God had said what the human being should be. The rabbi was the human being in God's image. That, to be sure, is why (but merely by the way) what the rabbi said about the meaning of Scripture derived from revelation. Collections of the things he said about Scripture constituted compositions integral to the Torah.

So in the rabbi, the word of God was made flesh. And out of the union of man and Torah, producing the rabbi as Torah incarnate, was born Judaism, the faith of Torah: the ever-present revelation, and always-open canon. For fifteen hundred years, from the time of the first collections of scriptural exegeses to our own day, the enduring context for *midrash* remained the same: encounter with the living God.

Index of
Names and Subjects

Index of
Biblical and Talmudic References